What Others Are Saying…

"In his first book, *Inevitable and Imminent*, Dr. Carrington makes a strong evangelical case that the central task of effective churches is grounded in the church's prayer life. But this is not easily achieved and is even harder to maintain. In this new volume, *The Church@Prayer: 52 Weeks at the Throne of Grace*, Carrington offers a methodology for maintaining that commitment with weekly reflections on biblical texts that directly address prayer's centrality and offers space for personal or corporate reflection within its pages. His message is simple, yet challenging; prayer works, prayer is work, and prayer leads to work. One senses from its pages Carrington's profound commitment to prayer's efficacy and its potential to transform this broken world of ours."

—The Rev William Weisenbach, D.Min., DD
Retired Presbyterian Minister
Former Professor of Practice Theology and
Vice President for Academic Affairs at
New York Theological Seminary

"The title, *The Church@Prayer: 52 Weeks at the Throne of Grace*, says it all. This volume on prayer is an amazing gem for any church to use in their weekly prayer meetings at such a time as this. Dr. Carrington, you have chosen to amplify the most powerful gift that God has given to us to unlock the power of heaven's storehouse. May God continue to bless you as you share your gift and thoughts with the world."

—Elder Flossie Lazarus

"Thank you for giving me this amazing opportunity to read and process this wonderful book. The great paradox is that, while I found your musings to be quite inspiring, I also found them to be incredibly convicting. No pastor, church leader, believer, or individual who is serious about growing their spiritual relationship with God can read this book and not be encouraged to invest more effort in prayer. I believe *The Church@Prayer: 52 Weeks at the Throne of Grace* should be a handbook for every church and a guide for starting a serious journey into the efficacy of prayer. My prayer is that this volume will become the launching pad of the revival that is so greatly needed in our world today. But that revival must be started by the church at prayer. Thanks again for this wonderful resource."

—Hugh Marriott, D.Min.
Pastor Allen Temple AME Church
Adjunct Professor, Long Island University

"*The Church@Prayer: 52 Weeks at the Throne of Grace* is a treasure chest of prayer gems for spiritual leaders who are seeking to transform their churches into houses of prayer. With 52 inspiring essays on prayer and thought-provoking discussion questions, this volume is the perfect guide for planning prayer-focused prayer meetings for an entire year. I admire how Dr. Carrington adeptly extracts insightful concepts on prayer from familiar (and some unlikely) Bible passages and presents practical life applications. Church leaders who embrace Dr. Carrington's bold challenge to spend *52 Weeks at the Throne of Grace* will experience the transforming power of prayer in their lives and a spiritual revival in their church."

—HAROLD GADIARE
FIRST ELDER
HANSON PLACE SDA CHURCH

"As I began to read *The Church@Prayer: 52 Weeks at the Throne of Grace*, I was quickly reminded of just how far some of our churches have strayed from the biblical model Christ gave us about the importance of prayer. I can literally feel the presence of the Holy Spirit in the bold convictions that Dr. Carrington asserts throughout these pages. As a church, we must now allow Christ to revive our spiritual condition. And when we pray with purpose, the church will come forth again, just as Lazarus did when Jesus called him forth from the grave. Amazing! You'll have to get the book and read that essay to find out how that can actually happen. This book is truly a must-read for all spiritual leaders who desire to put first things first: prayer."

—MITHRA WILLIAMS
DIRECTOR
SOUTHEASTERN CONFERENCE SDA PRAYER MINISTRIES

"Church cannot continue as usual! The impetus for change and survival is powerfully outlined in *The Church@Prayer: 52 Weeks at the Throne of Grace*. In this inspirational and instructive volume, Dr. H. W. Carrington provides compelling evidence and "out-of-the-box" thinking to propel today's church to success in its mission. By putting first things first, prayer can regain the primacy it was intended to have in the church of Christ. A renewed commitment to prayer is possible! Such an intervention will strengthen the church for success in this age and beyond. The challenge has been issued; I pray that the strategy outlined in this book will be implemented at the personal and congregational level by God's people to affect a finished work."

—SELWYN CARRINGTON, MD., PH.D.
CEO/HEALTH EDUCATOR
BRIDGE TO LIFE MINISTRIES, INC.

"It's interesting how Dr. Carrington went straight at the cancer and not the symptom of it in dealing with the spiritual morbidity within the Christian church. Thereafter, he places the church on a path to recovery and spiritual well-being for fifty-two weeks. *The Church@ Prayer: 52 Weeks at the Throne of Grace* highlights how the church has perhaps been doing everything right and one thing wrong—little or serious lack of the discipline of prayer. This is the reason for the cancer. Dr. Carrington cogently illustrates the diminishing returns from such a practice. I particularly like how he connects the theory and praxis of the discipline of prayer—each week being a link in a golden chain. And this chain remains as strong as each link remains unbroken. *The Church@Prayer* is a great work that promises transformational benefits both personally and for the corporate church."

—AINSWORTH E. JOSEPH, PH.D., D.MIN.
MINISTERIAL DIRECTOR
NORTHEASTERN CONFERENCE OF SEVENTH-DAY ADVENTISTS

"Another must-read book on prayer by my good friend, Dr. Hugh Wesley Carrington! As the Prayer Ministry Coordinator for our church, I found the devotional readings in *The Church@Prayer: 52 Weeks at the Throne of Grace* thought-provoking and inspiring. The contents are practical tools that can be used in your personal devotions and/or for group discussions. Especially valuable are the sections at the conclusion of each reading: What Are Your Thoughts? What Is Your Prayer? and the Discussion Questions. This format encourages readers to delve deeper into the readings, documenting their thoughts week after week throughout the year. No church leader, especially those in prayer ministry, should be without this valuable devotional."

—ELIES L. WHITFIELD, MSN, RN
PRAYER MINISTRY COORDINATOR, HANSON PLACE SDA CHURCH
ADJUNCT PROFESSOR, CUNY

"This time, there is no excuse for not having the resources and the reservoir full to focus on pray throughout the year—52 weeks. In his newest book, *The Church@Prayer: 52 Weeks at the Throne of Grace*, Hugh Wesley Carrington shares timeless wisdom into how an individual and church can remain connected, through prayer, to the throne of grace. For 52 weeks he'll keep you connected to the greatest hotspot the world has ever known. When you are sincerely and consistently connected through prayer to the throne of grace, you'll experience transformative power to sustain you through life's journey."

—CEDRIC N. BELCHER, SR.
AUTHOR: MORE: WHEN SUFFICIENT IS NOT ENOUGH
LEAD PASTOR, GRACE TEMPLE SDA CHURCH

"Never underestimate the power of prayer! In his new book, *The Church@Prayer: 52 Weeks at the Throne of Grace*, Dr. Hugh Wesley Carrington uses powerful Scriptures to take you on a 52-week prayer-filled, spiritual journey. Week after week you are blessed with edifying essays and thought-provoking discussion questions that encourage you to explore the supernatural power of prayer. Dr. Carrington's innovative and creative way of approaching this topic will keep you engaged throughout the year and beyond. *The Church@Prayer* is a must read for any group or individual looking to experience the life-changing power of prayer."

—DUANE S. BALDWIN
ELDER
BREATH OF LIFE FELLOWSHIP SDA CHURCH

"Pray without ceasing! There is power in prayer! Dr. Hugh Wesley Carrington reignites the passion and the desperate need for prayer within the Christian church. In *The Church@Prayer: 52 Weeks at the Throne of Grace*, Carrington emphasizes how prayer may be used as a vehicle through which spiritual growth may be achieved. Our success as a whole lies in a solid spiritual foundation that is based on prayer and the careful studying of God's Word. Prayer changes people and makes the impossible possible! Dr. Carrington explores how prayer provides us with the spiritual foresight needed to optimize the reach of our ministry. *The Church@Prayer: 52 Weeks at the Throne of Grace* is a must read! Once again, as with his other book, Dr. Carrington revolutionizes and takes the concept of prayer within the church to new heights. His take on prayer is innovative and refreshing!"

—WALTON ROSE, D.MIN.
SENIOR PASTOR
GOSHEN TEMPLE SDA CHURCH

"Just reading the table of contents confirmed for me that this will be a powerful book for anyone or any church who wants to improve their prayer life. *The Church@Prayer: 52 Weeks at the Throne of Grace* is practical and insightful. The prayer journey over the 52 weeks is mind-blowing, and your current understanding of what it means to truly pray will be tested along the way. I'm convinced that as you read, you'll find a favorite essay. Mine is *"Praying for a Second Chance."* This essay really touched my heart because indeed we're all in need of a second chance. You cannot go wrong by seriously reading and applying the spiritual and practical principles of this book!"

—SEAN ANDERSON, MDIV
ASSISTANT PASTOR
HANSON PLACE SDA CHURCH

"As an author and presenter who has both written and presented countless seminars and literatures on prayer, I highly endorse this book. Having witnessed the drought of prayer in churches, this book is an antidote as well as a guide for calling the church back to prayer. It takes away the excuses by providing practical and in-depth, thought-provoking content on the ministry of prayer to the individual and church alike. This book is needed in every minister's and every professed prayer teacher's literary collection. Having read countless books on prayer, I was intrigued by the approach on the subject that still brings fresh light and perspective to the subject. *The Church@Prayer: 52 Weeks at the Throne of Grace* will arouse the need for praying more, increase confidence in approaching God, and encourage stronger spiritual leadership among prayer educators and leaders.

—JOSIAN FRAMPTON
PASTOR, AUTHOR, SPEAKER, & SPIRITUAL/LIFE COACH
HE LEADETH ME MINISTRIES

"Dr. Carrington has been immersed in advancing the preeminent spiritual discipline for Christian disciples: prayer. His latest contribution is superb. In this new work, he calls us to refocus and reprioritize prayer, the ultimate spiritual discipline of discipleship. He ably illustrates the success that will come and the victories that will be won when prayer becomes a *sine qua non* for followers of Jesus. Dr. Carrington has found another way to aid you in your focus on prayer. *The Church@Prayer: 52 Weeks at the Throne of Grace* is user friendly and allows you to document your thoughts as you read. It provides thought-provoking introspective questions, and you'll find a rich buffet of biblical resources and references to take your prayer life to another level. Wow, fifty-two weeks with a focus each week on prayer! Watch what God will do for you as you embrace the journey now made much easier by the dedicated work of Dr. Carrington. He has made it possible for you to become the prayer warrior you need to be. This is a must read and a spiritual tool for everyone seeking growth in their prayer life."

—MAX FERGUSON, D.MIN.
PASTOR
SHILOH SDA CHURCH (PETERSBURG, VA)

The Church @Prayer:
52 Weeks at the Throne of Grace

Hugh Wesley Carrington, Ph.D.

BRIDGE PRESS INC.

The Church@Prayer

Copyright © 2020 by Hugh Wesley Carrington, Ph.D.

Published by Bridge Press, Inc., a division of Bridge, Inc., 46 Wildwood Road, Stamford, CT 06903

All rights reserved.

Printed in the United States of America on recycled paper.

Library of Congress Control Number: 2020910029
Hardcover ISBN: 978-1-7326132-1-8
Paperback ISBN: 978-1-7326132-2-5
e-Book ISBN: 978-1-7326132-0-1

Bible References

Common English Bible (CEB) copyright © 2011 Common English Bible. All rights reserved.

Contemporary English Version® (CEV) copyright © 1995 American Bible Society. All rights reserved.

The Good News Translation (GNT) copyright © 1976 by the American Bible Society.

King James Version (KJV), Public Domain.

Scripture taken from the Message (MSG). Copyright © 1993, 1994, 1995, 1996, 2000, 2001, 2002. Navpress Publishing Group. All rights reserved.

The Holy Bible, New International Version®, NIV® copyright © 1973, 1978, 1984, 2011 by Biblica, Inc.® All rights reserved worldwide.

Scripture taken from the New King James Version®. (NKJV) copyright © 1982 by Thomas Nelson, Inc. All rights reserved.

Holy Bible, New Living Translation (NLT) copyright © 1996, 2004, 2015 by Tyndale House Foundation. All rights reserved.

The Living Bible (TLB) copyright © 1971 by Tyndale House Foundation. All rights reserved.

This book is dedicated to all houses of prayer.

Spiritual matters are spiritually discerned; before you begin and while you're reading, pray for spiritual discernment.

Contents

Acknowledgments — xiii

Introduction — xv

MONTH 1 — 1

Week 1   Back To Basics — 3

Week 2   The Church's Primary Function — 9

Week 3   Spiritual Waiting — 13

Week 4   Praying With Purpose — 17

Week 5   On Your Way to Pray — 25

MONTH 2 — 31

Week 6   Persistence in Prayer — 33

Week 7   Prayer and Consistent Praise — 37

Week 8   Prayer and Revelation of Jesus — 41

Week 9   Show Yourself to the Priests — 45

MONTH 3 — 51

Week 10   Progressive Prayer — 53

Week 11   Challenging God Through Prayer — 59

Week 12   A Closer Relationship — 65

Week 13   Connecting with the King — 69

MONTH 4	**75**
Week 14 Temples of Prayer	77
Week 15 Remarkable Secrets	83
Week 16 Instructions Included	87
Week 17 A Straight Line	93
MONTH 5	**99**
Week 18 Two or Three: Families and Prayer	101
Week 19 I've Heard Your Request	105
Week 20 The Blessings of Intercessory Prayer	111
Week 21 Get on the Wall	115
Week 22 A Quiet and Peaceful Life	121
MONTH 6	**127**
Week 23 Thy Will Be Done	129
Week 24 No Glory	135
Week 25 After the High	141
Week 26 What Are You Hungry for?	147
MONTH 7	**153**
Week 27 You Gotta Sing!	155
Week 28 Show Me Your Glory	159
Week 29 In That Moment	165
Week 30 Tear Up the Roof	171
Week 31 Sweet-Smelling Incense	177
MONTH 8	**183**
Week 32 Praying for a Second Chance	185

Week 33	You Have Not	191
Week 34	Start Praying!	197
Week 35	When, If, and Then	203

MONTH 9 — 209

Week 36	Fully Armed, but Prayerless	211
Week 37	The Progression of Sin	219
Week 38	Delivered?	225
Week 39	Wait for It	231

MONTH 10 — 239

Week 40	I'm Only Human	241
Week 41	Where Is the Answer?	247
Week 42	Just Say the Word	253
Week 43	Only by Prayer	259
Week 44	God Still Delivers	265

MONTH 11 — 271

Week 45	Neglected Opportunity	273
Week 46	Transformation Through Prayer	279
Week 47	Prayer and Ministry	283
Week 48	It's Harvest Time	289

MONTH 12 — 295

Week 49	Send Me	297
Week 50	An End of Praying	303
Week 51	Prayer Must Give Way to Action	309
Week 52	I've Prayed, Now What?	315

BONUS ESSAY	**323**
Same God!	325
House of Prayer Indicator Assessment	333
Notes to the Reader	345
About the Author	349

Acknowledgments

A huge thank you to the many individuals, churches, and organizations that I've had the privilege to partner with over the last few years. Please know that many of the essays included in this volume were developed and/or refined after spending time with you in ministry. For the many times you've inspired me to go deeper, higher and wider in prayer, I will always be grateful.

Introduction

I love and welcome a good challenge. Moreover, I like to challenge myself. One evening several years ago after a prayer meeting at my local church, I challenged a church leader about making prayer the focus of our prayer meetings. The response? "Well, you'll just be talking about the same things every week." This seasoned spiritual leader was not alone in his thinking. Many spiritual leaders and members believe that a church cannot and will not focus on prayer for 52 weeks—one full year. As a matter of fact, one pastor was emphatic in his position: "It will never happen."

Are you struggling with planning your prayer meetings? Are you thinking there's no way you can study and discuss prayer for 52 weeks? Yes, you can! This 52 Weeks of Prayer Initiative (52-WPI) is just what you and your congregation needs. *The Church@ Prayer: 52 Weeks at the Throne of Grace* is a practical guide containing 52 essays on prayer that considers crucial concepts on the transforming influence of prayer and can be used to guide your prayer meeting discussions and sermon themes throughout the year.

These essays are not conclusive but are the author's spiritual musings on each passage of Scripture as seen through the eyes of prayer. As such, the essays were not written to cover every aspect of the specific theme; rather, they are intended to be used, along with the discussion questions, as a catalyst for the expression of the reader's thoughts and to encourage further dialogue.

Now you (your church) have more tools available to focus on prayer each week for the next year. I challenged myself to write these essays, and I'm currently challenging any new pastor to a church to spend the first 52 weeks of his tenure preaching and teaching about prayer. The challenge is also for any pastor—begin now by committing the next 52 weeks to preach and teach about prayer. Being intentional about prayer will set a tone for the congregation and unleash a tremendous wave of power to move that church forward spiritually.

I'm not a pastor, and I've never pastored a church, so I've never had the opportunity to implement this bold philosophy. But I am a Christian, and I've experienced the tremendous power of prayer. As such, I'm currently challenging spiritual leaders to try it. Spiritual leaders, this is your opportunity to engage your members over the next 52 weeks in practical prayer discussions that will foster ministries, programs, and activities to cultivate a house of prayer. I'm curious to see what God is going to do. What do you have to lose?

In my first book, *Inevitable & Imminent: On Becoming a House of Prayer—The Process*, I outlined the process of how a church becomes a house of prayer. This book allows you to do "it" for a full year. The subject matter experts tell us that most habits can be formed in 21 to 30 days; watch what happens to your church and in your home after these 52 weeks!

MONTH 1

Week 1
Back To Basics

"We ourselves, then, will give our full time to prayer and the work of preaching."

—Acts 6:4 (GNT)

It's a perplexing directive to tell someone at the beginning of a process or phase to go back. As we begin this new year, that's exactly what I want you to do, however. We didn't like it when our parents sent us back to comb our hair. We didn't like it when teachers sent us back to re-write that sentence. As adults, we don't like it when managers send us back to re-work the numbers or the report. We don't like to go back. But sometimes it's necessary to go back. Sometimes you have to go back to move forward. At some point in life, it may be necessary to take a few steps backwards, steady yourself, and then move forward.

I want you to get back to basics—individually and collectively as a church. I want you to go back and create a context for prayer or more prayer in your church. Doing so will position you (individually and collectively as a church) for tremendous spiritual growth in this new year. There are mind-blowing, spiritual benefits accessible to any individual or church that's willing to go back to basics. The individual or church that's willing to go back and do the things that God has called us to do will always experience success in ministry.

After all of their spiritual success, the newly developed church found itself at a crossroads—continue business as usual or go back to what produced success. The leaders of the early church, as noted in the focus text at the beginning, made a conscious decision to refocus and go back to prayer and preaching. Too often we experience success and we get distracted and neglect to continue with what produced the success. We get involved in ministries in which we should not be involved. Why? Because "everyone else is doing it." We continually place our emphasis on the wrong things and in the wrong areas. Consequently, the wrong things and the wrong areas are becoming our focus while prayer and preaching is pushed aside.[1]

The narrative found in Acts 6:1-8 is an amazing example from Scripture of a church that went back to basics and how they gained spiritually from the decision. The church is growing, the needs are many, and some group at the community services center is looking out for their friends and family members only. Wherever there's growth, there will always be increased opportunity for murmuring or arguments—more people = more strife. Whenever God's church begins to grow, individuals will allow the Devil to use them. This was not a simple matter; it was a spiritual matter—the church itself was at stake. This situation, if not addressed promptly, would impact spiritual, membership, financial, and ultimately kingdom growth.

The apostles called a meeting and told the church that they would not neglect ministry to serve tables. In other words, spiritual work is not the same as social work. Providing individuals daily bread is not the same as supplying them with the bread of life. Don't neglect ministry—ministry of the Word of God—for anyone or anything. When we don't do what we've been called to do, it will have a tremendous negative impact on the church and the work of the church—saving souls. This was more so a spiritual matter disguised as a social matter.

The proposed solution was to select seven men who would be responsible for this task while the apostles focused on prayer and preaching—back to basics. Serving tables was meaningful work, but it was a distraction from the main thing. It was a distraction from doing what had taken them to their spiritual zenith. Again, meeting spiritual needs is not the same as meeting social needs. Each has its place, but as a church, the main thing must be your main thing.

When we compare this experience in Acts with what is currently happening in some of our churches, we can appreciate the significance of going back to basics. When everything else has failed, we must go back to basics. Success in social, emotional, and physical matters can only come from a solid spiritual foundation of prayer and Bible study. Let's get back to basics and devote ourselves to sincere prayer that will lead to powerful and effective preaching—our central calling. This—prayer and preaching—is the main thing.

Let me share with you five consequences that will ensue when you get back to basics and rediscover your purpose. These five consequences will also happen when you focus on prayer and preaching of the Word.

First, you're actually going to do what you were called to do. Verse 6 says, "These men were brought to the apostles. Then the apostles prayed and placed their hands on the men to show that they had been chosen to do this work." The apostles actually did what they were called to do when they prayed. You must do the same.

Second, the Word of God will spread. Verse 7 simply says, "So the word of God spread." The Word of God prospered, the message of God kept on growing and spreading. We will speak to God in prayer, and He will speak to His people through our preaching; consequently, the Word of God will spread. When you get back to basics, the Word of God will spread.

Third, your church membership will grow. Verse 7 says, "...many more people in Jerusalem became followers." When you get back to basics, you'll experience tremendous membership growth.

Fourth, your spiritual leaders will finally believe. Verse 7 continues, "...and priests believed and obeyed, a large group of priests became obedient to the faith." Spiritual leaders were being spiritual leaders—doing what God had called them to do. When you get back to basics, your spiritual leaders will finally believe.

Fifth, you'll have power to do miracles. Verse 8 says, "God gave Stephen the power to work great miracles and wonders among the people." Here was a man called to work in community services and now he's performing miracles and wonders. When you get back to basics, you'll have power to execute modern-day miracles.

As I said earlier, this was not simply a matter of food distribution. This was not simply about Greek-speaking believers fighting with Hebrew-speaking believers. It wasn't only about unity. Something greater was at stake. This was a much larger problem; it was a spiritual problem that could have derailed the entire church. It was about the spiritual growth and development of the church.

Let's get back to basics and unleash the awesome power of God. Let's get back to sincere praying and righteous preaching. Let's get back to basics!

My Prayer

Father, I pray that we will be willing to always do what You've called us to do first. Amen.

What Are Your Thoughts?

What is Your Prayer?

Discussion Questions

1. Why is prayer so important when providing both daily bread and the bread of life?

2. Is it wrong for our spiritual leaders to make prayer and preaching their priority?

3. How does a lack of prayer and preaching affect the spiritual growth and development of a church?

Notes

[1] Hugh Wesley Carrington, *Inevitable and Imminent: On Becoming a House of Prayer—The Process* (Brooklyn: Bridge Press, 2015), 45.

WEEK 2

THE CHURCH'S PRIMARY FUNCTION

*And said unto them, It is written,
My house shall be called the house of prayer;
but ye have made it a den of thieves.*

—Matthew 21:13 (KJV)

For many Christian churches, Matthew 28:19 (KJV), "Go ye therefore, and teach all nations, baptizing them in the name of the Father, and of the Son, and of the Holy Ghost," is known as the Great Commission. I've been a Christian all my life, and I've never attended a church where this directive was not supported as the chief work of the church. All members of the church are called to go and disciple others (friends, family members) so that they can come to know Christ as Lord and Savior. Sound familiar?

While global teaching and baptizing is an important work of the church, it is not the primary function of the church. "No, then why are we here?" Glad you asked! The church's primary function, first and foremost, is to be a house of prayer. If the church fails at being a house of prayer, it will eventually fail at everything else.

Comparably, the human body has many organs (body parts) all with vital responsibilities to ensure proper functioning. However, I think that you would agree with me that the heart is the primary organ in our bodies. In both cases there is only one primary activity, prayer or a beating heart, which allows the church to fulfill its mission and the body to survive, respectively.

Herein is the pattern that established the primacy of prayer in the church. Notice that it was after prayer, one accord (Acts 1:14) and the outpouring of the Holy Spirit (Acts 2:4) that souls were won to the church (Acts 2:41)—the teaching and baptizing occurred after prayer. Christ did not send the remaining disciples out to conduct evangelism, distribute literature, develop health and wellness programs, children's outreach ministries, and marriage ministries first—without prayer. However, we often do all these things prior to praying. Jesus said to His disciples pray (Matthew 9:38), and then He sent them out (Matthew 10:5).

Christ was self-assured in our future results when He said, "my house shall be called the house of prayer." As such, He wants us to first pray and to know unequivocally that the ministries and subsequent soul winning will follow. If we don't make prayer the primary function of the church, all our ministries will ultimately fail, and we will never be able to fulfill the Great Commission.

My Prayer

Father, I pray that You will give us the spiritual foresight to see the pattern for optimal ministry. Thank You for this opportunity to co-labor with You. Amen.

THE CHURCH'S PRIMARY FUNCTION

What Are Your Thoughts?

_____
_____
_____
_____
_____
_____
_____
_____
_____
_____
_____
_____
_____
_____
_____
_____
_____
_____

What Is Your Prayer?

_____
_____
_____

Discussion Questions

1 How can prayer be used to support the Great Commission?

2 Is the Great Commission in danger because the modern church has not prioritized prayer?

3 Is the sequence pray, and then go, an optimal and sustainable design for effective ministry?

Week 3

SPIRITUAL WAITING

These all continued with one accord in prayer and supplication..."

—Acts 1:14 (KJV)

Before His ascension, Jesus reminds the disciples that His Father would send them the Holy Spirit as promised (John 14:16 and 16:7).

A *promise* is "an assurance that one will do a particular thing or that a particular thing will happen." In other words, expectations are raised, and a state of readiness ensues. In the case of the disciples, expectations were raised of something great and rightfully so. Whenever God makes a promise, we should position ourselves for something great.

Some biblical (and most times our own) promises are conditional. Some specific criteria have to be met to ensure that the thing will get done and that it will happen. One of the explicit conditions or instructions associated with the promise of the Holy Spirit was for the disciples to wait (Acts 1:4). While the only condition was for them to wait, we should keep in mind that God does not like us to be idle while waiting. He said, "...occupy [do business] till I come" (Luke 19:13). Christ was extremely careful not to tell the disciples when the promise would be fulfilled. Similarly, we should always be in a state of readiness.

Hence the question: what do you do when you're waiting for the Holy Spirit? Answer: you pray! Prayer is one of the activities that positions and conditions us to receive the power needed to be co-laborers with Christ. For the expectant Christian, there is a tremendous difference between waiting and spiritual waiting. The expectancy of something great does not allow us to squander the moments while waiting.

Too many of us are waiting on God to move, but we're not willing to occupy until He performs for us. If God promises you anything, pray while you're waiting. There was no explicit requirement or directive stated by Jesus for the disciples to pray. Nevertheless, when we take a look at our focus text, we find the disciples praying. Why? Well, the natural by-product of spiritual waiting is prayer.

If you're spiritually waiting in anticipation of a promise from God, know that He will honor His Word. So, here is another question: when you get what was promised, what are you going to do with it? The Holy Spirit and subsequent power were not assured to the disciples in vain. The expectation was that they would use it—witness for Him (Acts 1:8).

God endorses us so that we can be a blessing to others, and in so doing, we'll lead these individuals to accept Christ. God will provide the Holy Spirit and accompanying power, but when He does, we're expected to do something with it. He expects us to assist Him in finishing His work. As you spiritually wait for the promised outpouring of the latter Holy Spirit, pray. Let's all continue with unity in prayer.

My Prayer

Lord, I pray that we will begin now to spiritually wait for the promised latter rain. Amen.

What Are Your Thoughts?

_____

What is Your Prayer?

Discussion Questions

1. Why is prayer the fundamental difference between waiting and spiritual waiting?

2. Why is it important for us to pray while we wait for the outpouring of the latter rain?

3. What is the relationship between our enthusiasm to witness and prayer?

Week 4
Praying With Purpose

*After he had said this, he called out in a
loud voice, "Lazarus, come out!"*

—John 11:43 (GNT)

We're in need of a revival—but not just any revival—a spiritual revival. As we look around, we see that humanity has lost its way. We've lost our spiritual compass. As a nation and as Christians, we've neglected God for too long and now we're dealing with the consequences. But a spiritual revival can turn the tide. A spiritual revival can right the ship. A spiritual revival is needed in our churches that will be the catalyst for positive change. A spiritual revival is needed among us so that our churches can once again point the way for humanity. This spiritual revival, however, cannot and should not be launched without prayer. Pray with purpose.

The act of resuscitation (CPR) is only performed on things that are dying or on things that are presumed dead. In other words, no one does CPR on (attempts to revive) someone who is alive and well; it's not necessary. So, when I propose that a spiritual revival is necessary, it means that something is dead or is dying. I'll allow you to read between the lines. God wants to revive us spiritually, but some of us unwittingly, and others knowingly, have signed a DNR (do not resuscitate) statement. We've signaled to God by the way we're living and by the way we're worshiping: "Lord, do not resuscitate." Consequently, some of our churches are dying; they're on spiritual life support with no hope of recovery. Other churches are already spiritually dead.

If you care, and I know you do, you're asking, "Why? Why are we dead or dying spiritually?" You're asking, "What has caused humanity and unfortunately some in the Christian community to squander our position with God?"

The answer? We're not praying. Our lack of praying and our inability to pray with purpose is preventing the needed revival in our society. As such we must pray with purpose. 2 Chronicles 7:14 provides a hint as to the solution: If my people, which are called by my name [Christians—you and me], shall humble themselves and pray, and seek my face, and turn from their wicked ways; then will I hear [prayers] from heaven, and will forgive their sin, and will heal their land.

If you have not prayed, don't try to heal, revive, or bring back to life anything that is dying or that is dead. The power for spiritual revival is found only in praying with purpose. Let me now use the narrative of Lazarus' illness, death, and subsequent revival to illustrate the importance of praying with purpose and the powerful results you'll experience when you begin with prayer.

Lazarus is a representation of the church (John 11). Lazarus is sick—not the flu or a common cold. Some of our churches are spiritually sick—seriously sick. So, his sisters sent word to Jesus, "Lord, the one you love is sick." Some of us are crying out, "Lord, this church that You love is spiritually sick." Jesus responded, "This sickness will not end in death—this is for God's glory." The purpose of this spiritual illness (what some of our churches are currently experiencing) is not to death. If you pray with purpose, God's name will be glorified.

Jesus stayed where He was for two more days. There was a purpose for His delay then as there is a purpose for the current delay of His second coming. "Now we will go back to Judea." "Our friend Lazarus is asleep, and I am going there to wake him up." Many of you have lost loved one who are asleep in Christ. But know that God also calls them friend and is coming very soon to wake them up. "Lord, if he is asleep, he will get better." Lazarus was dead, but they thought Jesus was talking only about sleep. Many of us see the current state of the church (pitiful, poor, blind, and naked) and we're not disturbed; we don't understand. "Lazarus is dead!" Some of our churches are spiritually dead.

When Jesus got to Bethany, he found that Lazarus had already been in the tomb for four days. Some of our churches are dead and buried; they've been in the grave for many years now. Martha said to Him, "Lord, if you had been here, my brother would not have died. But even now I know that God will do anything you ask."

Jesus told her, "Your brother will live again!" Similar, I affirm that the church will live again. Mary then said the same: "Lord, if you had been here, my brother would not have died." Like Mary, some of us didn't get the memo, and we're still concerned. "Lord, the church." His response is the same: "Pray with purpose and the church will live again."

Jesus finally got their attention, and He inquires, "Where have you put his body?" "Lord, come and you will see." Jesus started crying; Jesus wept. In like fashion, Jesus is crying (weeping) when He observes the current spiritual state of some of our churches. Jesus said to them: "Take away the stone." Take away the things preventing your church from becoming a house of prayer. Remove whatever is preventing your church from growing spiritually. Remove the things that are preventing your church from being revived.

Martha said, "Lord, you know that Lazarus has been dead four days, and there will be a bad smell." Lord, we've been doing it this way for years now, and it's going to really stink around here if we ask church members to change. Jesus said to them: "Didn't I tell you that if you had faith, you would see the glory of God?" In other words, do what I'm asking you to do, church! Pray with purpose, and you'll see My glory. So, they took away the stone.

Between verse 1 and verse 42 of John 11, there are four prayers and/or references to prayer. If you are going to revive anything or bring anything back to life that is dying or dead, you have to pray with purpose.

- ***First prayer*** (v. 3): "Lord, the one you love is sick." This simple but powerful statement was intercessory prayer. If you're appealing to Jesus on behalf of another person, you're praying. You're praying with purpose.

- ***Second prayer*** (v. 4): "This sickness will not end in death—this is for God's glory. You're saying: "Where is the prayer?" Here it is… To have made such a bold and powerful statement, Jesus must have prayed. I'll confirm it for you later but know that Jesus prayed with purpose.

- ***Third prayer*** (v. 22): "But even now I know that God will do anything you ask." Martha is saying to Jesus: "Now that You're here, I'm not sure what You're going to do, but whatever You do, pray with purpose. Begin by talking with Your Father, and He'll give You whatever You pray for."

- ***Fourth prayer*** (v. 41): After the stone had been rolled aside, Jesus looked up toward heaven and prayed, "Father, I thank you for answering my prayer." This was a prayer of thanksgiving. You're saying, "God hasn't done anything; why is He thanking Him?"

Jesus is preparing to revive Lazarus, and He's praying a prayer of thanksgiving? This seems a little strange until you go back to verse 4. When He heard this, Jesus said, "This sickness will not end in death—this is for God's glory." The messenger shows up and delivered the news. When He heard the news, at that moment, like Nehemiah (Nehemiah 2:4), Jesus prayed with purpose. There is no way He could have responded so boldly without the guarantee that He had made a request to His Father and that His Father had responded, "Yes, this will be for my glory." He began by praying with purpose for revival, and now in verse 41, He continues with a prayer of thanksgiving.

John tells us, "After the stone had been rolled aside, Jesus looked up toward heaven and prayed…" As previously noted, this was not His initial petition, but a prayer of thanksgiving. This was not His first time communicating with His Father. In other words, you can't wait until the stone has been removed to begin praying. You can't wait until it begins to smell. You can't wait until the stone has been removed to initiate praying for a revival.

When you're going to call the church back to life or aiming to revive the church spiritually, that can't be your first time praying. That's too late. You should have already established a relationship with Christ that will now allow you to respond with confidence; this current state of the church (pitiful, poor, blind, and naked) will not be its end. This church will live again! Begin with prayer, pray with purpose, and confidentially tell them to remove the stone.

Now He continues His prayer in verse 42 by saying, "I know that you always answer my prayers." In other words, this situation was not uncommon for them. "Father, You've heard Me before, and I know that You hear Me now. We've been here before; we've done this, so let's do it again." What faith! John tells us (v. 43), when Jesus had finished praying, He shouted, "Lazarus, come forth!" When you're finished praying, now you have power. Now you have power, through prayer, to cry out in faith "Come forth." It begins with purposeful prayer.

We believe, and wrongfully so, that we can begin with music, preaching, Bible study, seminars and workshops, or tithes and offerings to ignite the revival. If we put these things before prayer, we're not going to be successful. After we've prayed with purpose, we'll be able to cry out, "Church, come forth" and watch our churches come alive spiritually. The current spiritual state of some of our churches and the pending spiritual attacks demand that we pray with purpose and keep praying. Tell them to remove the stone. Call your church forth from the grave; this spiritual death is not the end. "Lazarus, come forth!"

My Prayer

Father, help us to truly understand the power of prayer and what praying with purpose will do. Amen.

What Are Your Thoughts?

_____

What is Your Prayer?

_____

Discussion Questions

1. Why is it that we attempt to kindle the revival with everything but prayer?

   _____
   _____
   _____

2. Can prayer and a revival in the church really impact changes in our society?

   _____
   _____
   _____

3. What is the current status of prayer and spirituality in our churches?

   _____
   _____
   _____

WEEK 5

ON YOUR WAY TO PRAY

Now it happened, as we went to prayer, that a certain slave girl possessed with a spirit of divination met us, who brought her masters much profit by fortune-telling. This girl followed Paul and us, and cried out, saying, "These men are the servants of the Most High God, who proclaim to us the way of salvation." And this she did for many days. But Paul, greatly annoyed, turned and said to the spirit, "I command you in the name of Jesus Christ to come out of her." And he came out that very hour.

—Acts 16:16-18 (NKJV)

Have you ever gone to do something and got distracted? You're on your way to water the plants, and the phone rings. You're drafting an e-mail, and your spouse ask you a question. You went to get a drink of water and saw the grape juice. You went to the mall to get a tie and ended up in the Apple store. You're on your way to read your Bible, and your favorite song starts playing. You're typing a text message, and your best friend FaceTimes you. You got distracted.

Someone has been trying to read this essay for the last few days, but he keeps getting distracted. It happened to someone yesterday, today, and will certainly happen to someone tomorrow. In our post-modern society with all of its stimuli, it has happened, or it will happen at some point to all of us. Going to pray does not insulate us from distractions. In the focus text, Paul and his companions were on their way to pray, and they got distracted.

First, recognize that whenever you go to pray (start a ministry, make personal spiritual improvements), the Devil will always meet you to distract you (v. 16). You've been trying to pray but can't seem to find the time. Why? You're being distracted. Don't be confused as to what is happening; the Devil and his associates will not allow you to go and pray unencumbered; they will always meet you to distract you.

Prayer is communication with God. Through prayer we connect with God, and we develop a meaningful relationship with Him. This is precisely what the Devil is attempting to keep us from doing. Like He did with Paul and his friends, the Devil will meet us and distract us from praying—communicating, connecting, and developing a meaningful relationship with God. Somehow, we think that when we go to pray, we can leave the Devil behind. He knows where we're going; however, and he will get there before we do. You're trying to pray, start a ministry, or make personal spiritual improvements, but the Devil knows where you're heading. He actually goes ahead of you and then plots along the way to distract you.

Second, know that the distractions placed in your life by the Devil will always bring you profit (v. 16). The Devil is crafty and will always use distractions that will bring us much profit. Taking that call allows you to catch up with an old friend. Responding to your spouse keeps you in good standing. Drinking the grape juice placates your taste buds. Getting that new smartphone improves your status. Listening to your favorite song makes you feel good. It brings us much profit.

The selected distractions are not and will never be random. The Devil will always design them to profit us in some way. We can't make the time to pray because we're trying to: finish school, engage a new friend, get that promotion at work, learn the safety features of the new car, care for an ill family member, keep up with the election coverage, maintain the marriage. These are all admirable activities and deeds that bring us much profit, but they can also be used as distractions to keep us from praying.

It's important to note that praying for relief, from the distractions of the Devil, is a practical spiritual solution. God is eager to respond to our prayers for such help. Nevertheless, whether intentionally or unconsciously some of us choose not to pray about the distractions. Why? Because we're profiting, like the slave girl's masters, from the many distractions.

Third, note that the Devil's distractions from prayer are not one-time events (v. 18). The distractions will not simple happen once or twice. The Devil and his associates will follow you around for many days—day after day. Time after time the distractions will keep coming as you're struggling to pray, to start that ministry, or to make personal spiritual improvements.

Again, don't be perplexed as to what is happening. The Devil is behind the distractions and he'll continue until you lose your focus. Remember, you were on your way to pray. But every time you go to pray, you'll remember you have homework to finish. Every time you go to pray, your supervisor will have a new deadline. Every time you go to pray, that ill family member will need your assistance. The distractions from prayer are not one-time occurrences but daily events.

Fourth, let me ask a question: Are you annoyed by the Devil's distractions (v.18)? Seriously, are you annoyed—greatly annoyed—by the distractions that the Devil continues to place in your life? As noted above, some of us have become "okay" with the distractions because we're profiting from them.

Paul and his companions were also profiting as the slave girl spoke the truth—"These men are the servants of the Most

High God, who proclaim to us the way of salvation." It was good (profitable) for them to hear such words of praise. Yet they were a distraction because it was hindering their work. Are you greatly annoyed that the Devil is distracting you from developing a meaningful relationship with God through prayer?

We have to be honest and acknowledge that some "profitable" activities are hindering our prayer life, and we're okay—not annoyed. Sometimes the activities that are most profitable to us in the physical realm are equally distracting in the spiritual realm. While we're gaining physical, socially, and/or emotionally from these activities, we're losing spiritually. This is why we should be annoyed—greatly annoyed.

Fifth, know that the Devil's distractions can only be overcome by calling on the name of Jesus (v. 18). We can be liberated from the Devil's distractions singly by prayer. That is what you were on your way to do, so do it. Like Paul, forget about the earthly profit and rebuke the Devil in the name of Jesus.

When we go prayerless while facing the Devil's many distractions, the distractions become a way of life; prayer becomes secondary. You've got to know that the Devil is meeting you, yes, you're profiting, but it's a distraction from prayer. The only thing (calling on the name of Jesus) that can save you from the distractions is the very thing the Devil wants to keep you from doing—that's praying.

There is power in the name of Jesus. When you pray and use the name of Jesus, you'll see improvements in your prayer life, more power in your ministry, and you'll experience positive changes in your spiritual life. When? Right away—"that very hour."

My Prayer

Father, help us to call on Your name whenever we're being distracted in prayer. Amen.

What Are Your Thoughts?

What is Your Prayer?

DISCUSSION QUESTIONS

1. How is it possible for an entire church to be distracted from focusing on prayer?

   _____

   _____

   _____

2. What are some ways we profit but lose spiritually because we're not praying?

   _____

   _____

   _____

3. How can prayer be the solution for a distraction that's designed to keep us from praying?

   _____

   _____

   _____

MONTH 2

Week 6
Persistence in Prayer

Never stop praying, especially for others.
Always pray by the power of the Spirit.
Stay alert and keep praying for God's people,

—Ephesians 6:18 (CEV)

Anyone—parent, teacher, coach, athlete, manager, leader—will tell you that persistence is a chief component to any accomplishment. What is persistence? It is "the quality that allows someone to continue doing something or trying to do something even though it is difficult." In short, persistence is about perseverance, determination, importunity, and insistence.

Keep in mind, however, that no one is persistent for the sake of just being persistent. In other words, wherever and whenever this quality is present, there is usually a reason(s) for it—the hopeful achievement of some goal. The parent or teacher who is resolute with that child, the coach and athlete who is unrelenting, the manager or leader who is determined with his/her staff are all persistent because there's an objective in mind. There is a purpose for the efforts—a goal to be achieved.

Persistence will often lead to success. It could happen today, tomorrow, or it could actually take years, but success in line with God's purpose for your life will occur. In much the same way, our persistence in prayer is to achieve a goal. When you're unrelenting in prayer, success is guaranteed. What is it that you would have God do for others or for you? Are you praying about it? Are you being persistent in prayer with God?

Jacob was resolute because he wanted God's blessing (Genesis 32:26). Hannah was determined because she coveted a son (1 Samuel 1:11). And the Canaanite mother was relentless because she desired deliverance (Matthew 15:25). They all had a clear objective in mind and persisted with God in prayer until He responded. When we analyze the details of the above narratives, we find that the Canaanite mother persisted for several minutes. Jacob struggled all night. And Hannah agonized with God for several years.

The key words—*never stop, always, stay,* and *keep*—in our focus text are very instructive for us as Christians. Remember, it is not about how long you persist in prayer; it is more about having a specific goal in focus—an unmet desire or need—and enough faith to never stop praying, to always pray, to stay praying, to keep praying. Whatever you, don't stop praying.

My Prayer

Father, I pray for a faith that will allow us to trust You fully while praying persistently for our needs, desires, and wants. Amen.

What Are Your Thoughts?

What is Your Prayer?

Discussion Questions

1. Will God hear and answer our prayer because we're more persistent than the next person?

2. Is there a specific length of time after which we should stop praying with persistence?

3. What should we do when persistence in prayer does not produce an answer to prayer?

Week 7

Prayer and Consistent Praise

As they began to sing and praise, the Lord set ambushes against the men of Ammon and Moab and Mount Seir who were invading Judah, and they were defeated,

—2 Chronicles 20:22 (NIV)

We live in a world of relationships where things and processes intersect. It is a world of interdependence and one of cause and effect. From a very early age, we're trained to process our work in this way and often find ourselves trying to answer "the chicken-or-the-egg" question. So, here is the more meaningful question: what is the relationship between praise and prayer? In other words, how do these two disciplines intersect? Are they interdependent? Is there a cause-and-effect relationship?

The Bible does say, "Ask, and it shall be given you" (Matthew 7:7). Accordingly, for many of us, the substance of the relationship between the two—praise and prayer—begins with the asking.

That is, it begins with prayer. Subsequently, when God answers our prayer, we're moved to praise Him. We ask, we receive, we praise. There is absolutely nothing wrong for a Christian to think this way. However, I would challenge us to consider praise first. Stephen Nielsen asserts, "without praise it is impossible to pray, and without prayer there is no true praise."[1]

Prayer and praise do intersect; there is interdependence; there is a cause-and-effect relationship. My purpose here is not to engage you in a philosophical prayer or praise (chicken or egg) debate. Think about your relationship with your spouse, child, co-worker, or employee, etc. The relationships that begin with praise are the most fruitful relationships. It is no different with Christ; He covets and is worthy of our praise. Why would we not establish our connection with God by, first, praising Him for His many blessings? Praise Him for what He's about to do.

This praise, however, cannot be a single sensational act. It is not the single act of praise that will profit us, but our consistent authentic praise; it is what the Lord requires. Here is a spiritual suggestion that will allow you to be victorious in every aspect of your life: start praising God! When Judah began to sing and praise, the Lord defeated their enemies. You praise Him, He'll bless you, and now you're encouraged to pray even more. When you begin to praise, God will move on your behalf. When He does move, you can't help but pray. It's an acute and glorious cycle. Try it!

My Prayer

Father, help us to praise You. May we recognize that in our praise, there is prayer, and in our praying, we praise You. Amen.

PRAYER AND CONSISTENT PRAISE

WHAT ARE YOUR THOUGHTS?

WHAT IS YOUR PRAYER?

Discussion Questions

1 What is so noteworthy about prayer that we must give God His praise first?

2 Why is it important that our praise and prayer to God be consistent?

3 What is the intersect between praise and prayer?

Notes

[1] Stephen Nielsen, *Basics of Prayer—Discovering What Prayer Really Is* (Morrisonville, NC: LuLu Press, Inc., 2011), 36.

Week 8

Prayer and Revelation of Jesus

*"God has blessed you, Simon, son of Jonah,"
Jesus said, "for my Father in heaven has personally
revealed this to you—this is not from any human source."*

—Matthew 16:17 (TLB)

Many of us know *of* Jesus, but we don't *know* Jesus. We know what others tell us about Him, what they say about Him, but we don't know Him for who He really is—Messiah, Savior, Christ, Son of the living God. One of the reasons we don't know Jesus is because we're not praying. If you don't communicate with individuals, becoming acquainted with them is really hard. There is a direct correlation between the time we spend in prayer and the revelation to us of Jesus—being able to say who He is.

In reading our focus text, many will ask: "Was Peter in prayer when God personally revealed to him that Jesus is Son of the living God?" The answer is no, but Peter was in the presence of God. I'm excited to remind you of this amazing fact: prayer puts us in the presence of God. Prayer is one of the ways to engage God to get this type of revelation. Prayer is the primer for knowledge of Jesus. If we take the time to pray, we will get to know Jesus. Why? Because prayer puts us in the presence of God and positions us for an amazing revelation.

In our current society, many of us have superficial relationships with those around us. I'm not blaming you—simply stating the facts. We're too busy, they're too busy, and we really don't communicate with each other. Hence, we don't get to know each other. When we genuinely communicate with others, we're more likely to get to know them better. Consequently, we're more likely to have a better relationship with them and hence, we'll disclose more information to each other.

Meaningful communication and relationship building is not one way. In other words, if you tell me you're communicating well with someone, that tells me dialogue is taking place—an exchange of information. Prayer in its simplest form of communication is communication with God. Accordingly, we observe the parallel between prayer and the revelation of Jesus. Through prayer: (1) we develop meaningful communication with God, (2) we get to know Him better, and (3) He'll disclose information to us.

While God is God and He can and will reveal Himself to whomever, whenever, wherever, and however, our lack of prayer impedes the process. As such, our attempts to share Jesus with others must begin with prayer. Individuals in our communities and churches will never know Jesus unless God reveals Himself to them. We cannot depend upon any human source for this revelation and knowledge. We are truly blessed when, through prayer, we get into the presence of God, and He condescends to reveal Jesus to us.

My Prayer

Father, as we enter Your presence through prayer, reveal Jesus—the Son of God—to us. Amen.

What Are Your Thoughts?

What is Your Prayer?

Discussion Questions

1. Why is getting into God's presence, through prayer, so important?

2. Can we really come to a true understanding of who God is through prayer?

3. Why is it important for us to pray and get to know Jesus before we attempt to share Him with others?

Week 9

Show Yourself to the Priests

...and called out in a loud voice, "Jesus, Master, have pity on us!" When he saw them, he said, "Go, show yourselves to the priests." And as they went, they were cleansed. One of them, when he saw he was healed, came back, praising God in a loud voice.

—Luke 17:13-15 (NIV)

To be connected means that things are joined or linked together. At times we may not want to acknowledge it, but we live in a very connected world. An earthquake in Japan can affect financial markets around the world. Similarly, a tsunami in Indonesia can impact the ecological systems of countries thousands of miles away. And many will remember the ripple effects throughout the world during the financial crisis of 2008 and the COVID-19 events of 2020. For the Christian, this connectedness is also present in the spiritual world. Someone has said that prayer and faith are Siamese twins.[1] When we add praise to the family, we get triplets.

Like most sets of siblings, where one is present, the others are typically nearby. Prayer, faith, and praise are joined and inseparable. They're connected and cannot survive without each other. Our level of praise is an indication of our level of faith, and our level of faith is a signal to the genuineness of our prayers. Our focus text is instructive as to the connectedness of these three concepts — prayer, faith, and praise.

Prayer: *"Jesus, Master, have pity on us!"* The Lord is trying to get our attention through the difficulties He sometimes place/allow in our lives. He is saying to us, "I can help! Talk to me, pray." Being afraid when confronted with a problem is a natural human emotion. Fear, however, should not consume the Christian's life. The Lord is trying to get our attention—stop and pray. Too often we do everything else but pray, and God is not pleased. Our problems, trials, issues, and concerns are not there just to make our lives miserable; they are a call for us to pray. Notice that the lepers' prayer was not for healing, but for pity—mercy. While our prayers should be specific, sometimes all we can do is cry out for God's mercy.

Faith: *And as they went, they were cleansed.* Occasionally, the answer to our prayers will come in the form of precise instructions, that if followed will yield the desired outcome. That's what I like about God; He does not leave us wondering; He is always very clear in what He wants us to do: "Go, show yourselves to the priests." You're saying to yourself: "I'm crying out for mercy, and You're sending me to the priest? This makes no sense."

Faith must allow us to act when directed by God. We can pray without ceasing, but sometimes the answer will not come until we demonstrate faith. It will take faith (obedience) to realize the desired answer. The priest was the only one who could officially certify and pronounce them clean. Sometimes, the answer to our prayer resides between our current situation and our act of faith. Know that your cry for mercy has been heard. You will be healed, but your faith must allow you to move.

Praise: *...came back, praising God in a loud voice.* Praise is important to God. "Were not all ten cleansed? Where are the other nine?" (v. 17). If you've ever wondered or questioned whether praise is important to God, these questions should confirm it. Troubles lose their significance and you gain a vision of the greatness of God when you're busy praising Him. When we engage in praise, by default it allows God to immediately move on our behalf. And what's impressive about the whole thing is that when He moves, He will move in supernatural, unbelievable, and mind-boggling ways.

The instructions were clear, yet one of the lepers deviated and came back to Christ. Amending the plan to say "thank you" to God is always permissible. While it may appear that this one leper was being disobedient, he actually placed himself in a most favorable position by returning to praise Christ. The instructions were very specific: "Go, show yourselves to the priests."

Who is Christ? He is our great High Priest. The power of prayer, faith, and praise is that it moves God to act on our behalf. Christ—the great High Priest—officially pronounced the leaper clean (v. 19).

My Prayer

Father, we show ourselves to Thee; pronounce us clean. Amen.

What Are Your Thoughts?

What is Your Prayer?

Discussion Questions

1 What does it mean to pray for God's mercy and not specific healing?

2 How does our prayerlessness prevent us from having faith when God says move?

3 Why does God move to answer our prayer when we praise Him?

Notes

[1] E. M. Bounds, *E. M. Bounds on Prayer* (New Kensington, Penn.: Whitaker House, 1997), 211.

Month 3

Week 10

Progressive Prayer

*And if we know that God listens when we pray,
we are sure that our prayers have already been answered.*

—1 John 5:15 (CEV)

During a sermon in January 2015, I expressed to a congregation that they should "stop praying about it and start praising God." I told them to tell God "this is the last time I'm praying about this. Going forward, I'm going to praise you." After conducting a workshop in March 2015, I received a question by e-mail asking about praying too much. I responded, "I don't know of any reason or circumstance where I would say that someone is praying too much. The Bible is clear about the amount of time we should spend in prayer; our lives should be lived in an attitude of prayer."

A few weeks later, I wrote an essay about the most difficult prayer—"thy will be done." I wrote about how Jesus prayed that prayer three times, and I challenged my readers with this statement: "Don't change or abandon your prayer unless or until God tells you 'I'm not going to answer that prayer.'"

Stop praying; start praising. There is no such thing as praying too much. Don't abandon your prayer. What am I saying? After reflecting on the above statements, I was somewhat perplexed, and I became concerned that I was contradicting myself and would also confuse others. I became even more concerned that God was contradicting Himself. Being the kind of God that He is, He quickly cleared it up. He revealed to me that He was not contradicting Himself and outlined a prayer sequence—progressive prayer.

Progressive means that something is happening or developing gradually or in stages. It is proceeding step by step, increasing in extent or severity. Progressive is an adjective. When used to modify prayer, it lets us know that prayer should develop, proceed step by step, and increase in extent or severity. Progressive prayer moves from asking, to praising, to thanksgiving. God was not contradicting Himself, and He answered my questions. I hope this explanation of progressive prayer addresses any questions you may have.

Our praying must be progressive; that means **asking**. Nothing is wrong with asking. God's Word is clear that we should ask—within His will—and we will receive (1 John 5:14). Too many of us, however, keep asking, but we fail to move beyond the asking. Some individuals keep praying but will never take any action—moving to the next level. When we pray, God will answer; the promise "you shall receive" is real. Nevertheless, a time comes when God expects us to stop asking and to start praising.

Knowing that God's promises are true, that He cannot and will not go back on His Word, should allow us to boldly move to the next level of prayer—***praising***. When I shared this concept of progressive prayer, one individual asked, "What am I praising God for?"

I answered, "You praise Him for what He's going to do. Your prayer has already been answered" (1 John 5:15).

She responded, "But He has not done anything."

I said, "We can be assured that however God decides to answer our prayer will be best for us, so just praise Him."

Making this transition can be difficult, but at some point, we have to stop asking and start praising Him. We're able to praise Him because the prayer is God-sanctioned. If you know that what you're asking for is the right request (within His will), praise Him now with confidence. Too many of us wait until we get the desired response and then we praise, but after God has answered our prayer is too late. Praising Him *after* is a different level of praying. I'll address that level of prayer next.

The final and highest level of progressive prayer is **thanksgiving**. You've asked Him, you've praised Him, and now you must thank Him for hearing and answering your prayer. First, you thank Him for hearing—God hears every prayer. Thank Him for taking the time to listen. Ultimately, you thank Him for answering the prayer. If you prayed for sunshine and He responded favorably, thank Him. If He responded with rain or snow, you still thank Him. Why? God knows best, and our expression of thanksgiving is acknowledgment of that humbling fact.

My Prayer

Father, help us to ask boldly, to praise with confidence, and to thank You nevertheless. Amen.

What Are Your Thoughts?

What is Your Prayer?

Discussion Questions

1. If our prayer has already been answered, why are we still praying?

   _____
   _____
   _____

2. What do we do if we've praised God and we still don't get what we've prayed for?

   _____
   _____
   _____

3. Why is it so difficult for us to get to thanksgiving—the highest form of prayer?

   _____
   _____
   _____

Week 11

Challenging God Through Prayer

"Come. Sit down. Let's argue this out..."

—Isaiah 1:18 (MSG)

When I was first introduced to the phrase "question authority," I added, "and then ask them why." In other words, challenge their response. I later discovered that this was dangerous and destructive behavior (Coles, 1996).[1] This method of questioning authority, some have argued, can result in widespread dysfunctionality. While it can and does enhance a person's self-interest, it greatly weakens his/her ability to cooperate with others (Potter and Estren, 2012).[2]

So, in the context of questioning authority, what does it mean to challenge God? Is it bad to challenge God? Well, He did say, "Come now, and let us reason [*argue, settle this thing*] together..." (Isaiah 1:18). He further said, "...prove [test, try] me now herewith, if I will not open you the windows..." (Malachi 3:10). A challenge is "the act or process of provoking or testing."

This could be with a stimulating task or problem. It can also be an objection or query as to the truth of something, often with an implicit demand for proof. As sinful humans, we don't like to be challenged. God, however, does not mind our challenges. Respectfully challenging God is not a sin.

It is difficult to test someone who knows everything and already has an answer prepared. How do we challenge a God who already knows everything? He said, "before they call, I will answer; and while they are yet speaking, I will hear" (Isaiah 65:24). God actually looks forward to our challenges because it allows Him to show up and show off. So how do we humbly challenge God? We challenge Him through our prayers. Challenging God through prayer is not dangerous and destructive behavior. It's not questioning His authority. What we're doing is simply asking Him to honor His promises. Most of us are praying, but we're not challenging God.

Allow me to share two examples from Scripture of individuals who challenged God through prayer. First, God covenanted with Moses to take the children of Israel into the Promised Land. But now He reveals to Moses that He's disposed to destroy them all because of their disobedience (Numbers 14:12). Nevertheless, Moses challenged God to keep His promise. He said to God, "The Egyptians will say the Lord had to kill them because he wasn't able to take care of them in the wilderness" (v. 16).

Second, God promised Abraham that the number of his children will be like the sand of the sea. David reminds us that God is fair and just (Psalm 25:8). As with Moses, God reveals to Abraham that He will destroy Sodom and Gomorrah because of their wicked ways (Genesis 18:20). Similarly, Abraham challenged God. He said to Him, "Are you serious? Are you planning on getting rid of the good people right along with the bad?" (v. 23).

We too can and must challenge God through prayer. If we develop and maintain a meaningful relationship with Christ, like Moses, Abraham, and others did, God will also reveal His plans to us. He will share His plans, giving us an opportunity to counter—to challenge Him. Herein lies the problem, however; we can't hear His voice. We often don't know what He has promised, and we're certainly not praying.

The only way for us to *reason* (argue, settle this thing), *prove* (test, try), or *challenge* God is through prayer. "This is the sure way of prevailing with the Lord in prayer. We may humbly remind Him of what He has said."[3] Anything else is dangerous and destructive behavior.

My Prayer

Father, thank You for allowing us to challenge You to keep Your promises. Amen.

What Are Your Thoughts?

_____
_____
_____
_____
_____
_____
_____
_____
_____
_____
_____
_____
_____
_____
_____
_____
_____
_____
_____

What is Your Prayer?

_____
_____
_____

Discussion Questions

1 What type of prayer relationship must we have with God to be able to challenge Him?

_____

_____

_____

2 How have you challenged God through prayer?

_____

_____

_____

3 What is the relationship between knowing God's promises and being able to challenge Him through prayer?

_____

_____

_____

Notes

[1] Robert Coles, *Remembering Timothy Leary* (MacNeil-Lehrer Productions; interview by Charlayne Hunter-Gault, Arlington, VA: NewsHour Productions, 1996).

[2] Beverly Potter and Mark Estren, *Question Authority: To Think for Yourself* (Berkeley, CA: Ronin Publishing, Inc., 2012), 23.

[3] Charles Spurgeon, *Faith's Checkbook—Daily Devotions* (https://www.lightsource.com/devotionals/faiths-checkbook-ch-spurgeon/faiths-checkbook-may-28-11541381.html), May 28.

Week 12

A Closer Relationship

I pray that they will all be one, just as you and I are one—as you are in me, Father, and I am in you...,

—John 17:21 (NLT)

On New Year's Eve 2015, I stood before our congregation to lead them in a season of prayer. My assignment was to encourage the church to pray for a closer relationship with Christ as we prepared to begin a new year. I began by asking two questions. First, "How many of you have prayed about/for a relationship with someone?" Second, "How many of you have prayed about your relationship with Christ—prayed desiring a closer, stronger, and more committed relationship with Him?"

As you reflect on those question, think back to elementary school, middle school, high school, college, or even just yesterday, and you'll be able to recall how you prayed that special person would accept your wooing. As we reflect, we can smile and laugh about it, now, but we really did pray. You'll be surprised, however, to know that many of us desire a closer relationship with Christ but have never taken the time to pray about it. We've not talked with Christ about having a closer relationship with Him. As we went to our knees on New Year's Eve, I encouraged the congregation to pray and ask for a closer relationship with Christ.

One of the best ways to begin and maintain a relationship with anyone is to speak with him or her. Again, remember when you met that person and you stayed up until 3:00, 4:00, or 5:00 in the morning—even when you had work/school the next day? I know, I'm bringing back too many memories. Nevertheless, it's a fact, relationships can only develop and become stronger through meaningful communication.

I can read all I want to about someone. I can watch shows and videos about the person. However, it does not mean that I have a relationship with that individual. But isn't that how we define the depth or existence of our relationship with Christ? Well, I read my Bible every day, and I often watch Christian movies and videos. Good start, but that's not enough. In our focus text, Jesus prayed for a closer relationship with His Father, and we must do the same.

Prayer (communication with God) is the means to build that closer relationship with Christ. It's not just about reading your Bible or watching Christian programs. While God has activities planned for the next morning, He will stay up with you as long as you like—pray. Jesus was one; He had an intimate relationship with the Father. And we must pray for the same type of relationship. Oh, to have a closer relationship with Christ!

My Prayer

Holy Father, we desire a closer relationship with You. I pray that we will seek, develop, and maintain a similar relationship with You as You have with Your Son. Amen.

What Are Your Thoughts?

What is Your Prayer?

Discussion Questions

1. How would you describe your prayer relationship with Christ?
   _____
   _____
   _____

2. Why is Bible study and watching Christian programs not enough to establish a prayer relationship with Christ?
   _____
   _____
   _____

3. Is it possible for us to have the kind of relationship that Jesus has with His Father through prayer?
   _____
   _____
   _____

WEEK 13

CONNECTING WITH THE KING

> *For all these things do the nations of the world seek after: and your Father knoweth that ye have need of these things. But rather seek ye the kingdom of God; and all these things shall be added unto you. Fear not, little flock; for it is your Father's good pleasure to give you the kingdom.*
>
> —LUKE 12:30-32 (KJV)

One of my pet peeves is wasting time. I become very annoyed with individuals who waste my time. Time is one of those commodities that we can never get back—don't waste it. When it comes to praying, some individuals see it as a waste of time. To them, they will never be able to get back time spent in prayer. In other words, "If God knows what I need, why do I need to pray? God, if you know I need it, just do it—give it to me. Don't waste my time." You may be surprised to learn that some individuals (even Christians) reason and function this way. Furthermore, some use Scripture to back up their thinking: "…your Father knoweth that ye have need of these things." And so, they reason: "God already knows what we need, so why pray? Let's not waste time."

On the other hand, some of us go to the other extreme. Think about it and be honest with yourself. We do our best to avoid friends and family members who constantly ask for things. We usually don't hear from these individuals until they need something. While God is not like us, He similarly takes no pleasure in our constant asking for things that He already knows that we need. Someone is saying, "See I told you—no need to pray." Still, if we see prayer as a way to get things, then we only pray when we need things.

Both perspectives noted above are incorrect. The purpose of prayer, conversely, is to connect to the King of the kingdom. If we connect with the King, we get the kingdom. The purposefulness of prayer is that it allows us to develop and maintain a connection with God. Prayer is not a waste of time. Neither is it simply an opportunity to beg God when we have needs. Prayer has to be, and it is much more.

Praying to God to develop and maintain a connection with Him instead of praying for things distinguishes us from the rest of the world. Our focus text is clear: "For all these things do the nations of the world seek after…." While everyone else is seeking after the "these things," Christians should be seeking after the thing that is most essential—the kingdom. Nothing is wrong with the "these things." Trust me, God knows that they are necessary. He knows that we have need of them, and He will provide them. Moreover, anything that God knows I need will be good for me.

A similar narrative is found in Matthew 6:25-33. However, Luke adds this comforting and amazing fact to his narrative. He notes, "…for it is your Father's good pleasure to give you the kingdom." Pause, don't rush past this promise! God wants to give us the kingdom. Like the rest of the world, some Christians are too busy praying for the "these things" (food, drink, clothes), when it is God's desire to give us the kingdom. When we connect with God through prayer, we're signaling to Him that we're seeking His kingdom. Remember, connect with the King and get the kingdom. The food, drink, and clothing will come; He sends sun and rain on the just and the unjust (Matthew 5:45). His kingdom, however, must be sought after—"…seek ye first the kingdom of God."

Why pray? We pray to stay connected to the One who takes pleasure in giving us the kingdom. Look toward His kingdom and the "these things" of this world will lose their significance. I challenge you to make His kingdom your priority by developing and maintaining a connection with God through prayer, and by default, He will feed, quench, and clothe you. American Express is correct; membership does have its privileges.

My Prayer

Father, we pray not for things, but for a closer walk with the King of the kingdom. Amen.

What Are Your Thoughts?

What is Your Prayer?

Discussion Questions

1 If God knows we need "things," why do we have to pray for them?

   _____

   _____

   _____

2 Why is it wise for us to pray for an improved relationship with Christ and not "things"?

   _____

   _____

   _____

3 What is the relationship between prayer (connecting with the King) and getting God's kingdom?

   _____

   _____

   _____

MONTH 4

Week 14
Temples of Prayer

"The Scriptures say my Temple is a place of prayer,"
he declared, "but you have turned it into a den of thieves."

—Matthew 21:13 (TLB)

In March 2015, I was invited to speak to a group of Christian men at their weekly meeting. I was in the process of completing the manuscript for my first book and had the privilege of presenting on the topic: "Prayer, Power, and Purpose." It was Monday evening, and these men could have been doing any number of things. But there we were, gathered in the church's fellowship hall studying Scripture. It was an awesome experience to stand before a group of men to present God's Word. I will always cherish the experience.

About seven slides into my presentation, I shared with them that Jesus made the proclamation in Matthew 21:13 that leads to our having power in our churches. As we talked, one of the group's leaders reminded me that we are the temple. It was a very meaningful point, and it stimulated my thoughts in relationship to our topic—prayer. I was able to complete my presentation but found myself meditating on the observation the next day and for several days after. God brought me back to it weeks later, and I wrote the following essay.

He was correct and Scripture is clear that we (our bodies) are temples of God. For example:

- "But Jesus was talking about his body as the Temple" – John 2:21 (MSG).
- "You realize, don't you, that you are the temple of God…?" – 1 Corinthians 3:16 (MSG).
- "What? Know ye not that your body is the temple of the Holy Ghost…?" – 1 Corinthians 6:19 (KJV).
- "…for ye are the temple of the living God" – 2 Corinthians 6:16 (KJV).

God possessed, occupied, and inhabited the ancient temple. It was where God communicated and revealed Himself to His people. In much the same pattern, He desires to speak and show Himself to each of us in the modern temple. He finds it difficult at times, however, because everything else is crowding Him out. This is why He had to clear the ancient temple (Matthew 21:12), and it is why He also wants us to clear our temples of distractions. As with the ancient temple, our temples can only be possessed, occupied, and inhabited by God if it is a place of prayer.

Yes, we are the temple—as such, the individual and the collective "we" should be a place of prayer. When Jesus made the declaration "…my Temple is a place of prayer" or "…my house shall be a house of prayer," He was talking about us being a place—a church of prayer. Everyone is an individual temple that comprises the collective temple—body, people, church. Here is another way we could read His proclamation: "My body is a place of prayer. My church/people shall be a church/people of prayer. I am a place of prayer."

My Prayer

Father, I pray that we will individually embrace our temple status and collectively become a church of prayer. Amen.

What Are Your Thoughts?

What is Your Prayer?

Discussion Questions

1. If we are temples of prayer, what should that say about our prayer lives?

2. How can we remove the things from the temple that is distracting us from prayer?

3. How does being a temple of prayer allow God to occupy us?

Week 15

Remarkable Secrets

*Ask me and I will tell you remarkable secrets you
do not know about things to come.*

—Jeremiah 33:3 (NLT)

A *secret* is "something kept from public knowledge or the knowledge of a specific person." It is something known only to a certain person or persons and purposely kept from the knowledge of others. Appropriately, secrets are called secrets for a reason; you're not supposed to know or share. Some individuals, organizations, and countries collectively spend billions of dollars each year to maintain their secrets. By the way, we still don't know Victoria's secret…

As already noted, a secret is purposely kept from the knowledge of others. In other words, if you're privileged to know the secret, you're not supposed to tell. Furthermore, if you're asked about the secret, again, you're not supposed to tell. In our focus text, God has absolutely no respect for these rules. He says, "Ask me and I will tell you…." Not only is He ready and willing to tell, He promises to reveal the "remarkable" secrets. We know that's the "one" secret all individuals are trying their best to protect.

You can relax; no scandals here. The secrets of God are not found in tabloids; it's not gossip. The secrets of God are about the great, mighty, unsearchable, wondrous things to come. Some individuals, organizations, and even countries are expending significant resources to keep us ignorant of these secrets. God, however, is ready and willing to share if we would ask. As praying Christians, we have full access to the remarkable secrets of things to come. As such, we should not live our lives in fear of the unknown.

Christians should know the remarkable secrets of how this world will end and of the beauty of the one to come. Moreover, we are under spiritual obligation to share these secrets. Sounds good. Here is the glitch: we're not praying. God cannot and will not reveal His secrets to those who are not praying. Therefore, He says, "Ask me and I will tell you…" Remember, the rule is clear: when you're asked about the secret, don't tell. Again, such practices do not apply to God—ask.

Charles Spurgeon encourages us to pray. He points out that God has wonders in store for us. What we have never seen, heard of, or dreamed of, He will do for us. He will invent new blessings if needful.[1] If you're expecting to know what's on God's mind, as all Christians should, you have to ask—you have to pray. Matthew Henry notes, "Promises are given, not to supersede, but to quicken and encourage prayer."[2] Too often we want to know, but we don't ask; we don't pray. If God has promised to tell you, you're fully within your rights to ask.

My Prayer

Father, we need to know, we want to know what's on Your mind. Help us to ask—help us to pray. Amen.

What Are Your Thoughts?

What is Your Prayer?

Discussion Questions

1. God has promised to tell. How should that promise impact our prayer lives?

2. Can it really be true that God will not reveal His secrets to those who are not praying?

3. What is it that we need to know and are willing to pray about?

Notes

[1] Charles Spurgeon, *Faith's Checkbook—Daily Devotions* https://www.oneplace.com/ministries/spurgeon-sermons/read/devotionals/faiths-checkbook-ch-spurgeon/faiths-checkbook-june-29-11545336.html), June 29.

[2] Matthew Henry, *Matthew Henry's Commentary on the Whole Bible*, (Peabody, Massachusetts: Hendrickson Publishers, 1991), 1295.

Week 16

Instructions Included

"If you ask me for anything in my name, I will do it."

—John 14:14 (GNT)

An *instruction* is "a statement that describes how to do something." Similarly, it can be an order or command. While most of us would not deny the importance of instructions, we're often guilty of not reading and/or following instructions. This potentially dangerous behavior is somewhat reinforced because things often work themselves out through trial and error; we never experience any major negative consequences. Nonetheless the outcome, we're forced to admit that when we read and follow instructions, we get the optimal or maximum benefits from the product or service.

In 2007, I bought a brand-new Samsung 46-inch flat panel television. I unpacked the television, plugged it in, and used the remote control to turn it on, never bothering to read the instructions. I never looked back until seven years later. In January 2014 I was asked to present a brief thought for prayer meeting. As I prepared my presentation, I was prompted by the Holy Spirit to reference my neglect to read and follow instructions for the proper operation of the remote control as an illustration. The point I was aiming to make? If we read and follow God's instructions, we're able to get the optimal or maximum benefits from prayer.

As mentioned, the television came with a remote control and instructions that I never read. On page 5 of the Instruction Manual, right up front, were the instructions for proper use of the remote to get optimal or maximum benefit. For example:

- When using the remote, always point it **directly** at the TV.
- The remote control can be used up to a **distance** of 23 feet from the TV.
- You can use the remote control to **activate** your VCR, cable box, and DVD player.

These instructions seem to be very straightforward, and they are. Everyone knows that you can't be around the corner or point the remote at the fish tank and expect it to control the television. So, what's the big deal? The television was working fine; I was able to watch sports and movies. But the question remains: was I getting the optimal or maximum benefits from that brand-new 46-inch flat panel television? In our focus text, Christ provided some specific instructions about prayer. If read and followed, our lives would be much better; we would get the optimal or maximum benefits from prayer.

The first instruction—"ask me." Too often we find ourselves asking everyone else. We're on Facebook and Twitter telling and asking everyone else, when Christ's specific instructions are to *ask Him*. We say, "God is not concerned about me. He's not interested in answering my prayers." No, God is thinking about you, and He is willing to answer your prayers, but you have not asked. Furthermore, some of us are too proud to ask. We must learn to humble ourselves and pray—ask. When praying, we must be **direct** and ask Christ.

The second instruction is ask me—"for anything." Most of us categorize our problems or desires into three categories: mine, family and friends, and God's. We're limiting God by filtering our problems or desires and deciding what He can and cannot handle. What a foolish way to compartmentalize our lives when God is instructing us to challenge Him for anything! Our prayer, however, must be within His will—the ***distance*** is consequential. Some individuals find God's will to be restrictive. But we're limited, however, count it a privilege to be limited within God's limitless will.

Finally, He instructs us to ask for anything—"in my name." Watchman Nee notes, "The name of the Lord Jesus has become too common in human language."[1] Yet, there is still power in the name of Jesus. So, go ahead, name drop. Jesus is well known; tell them He sent you. Know without a doubt that in prayer, we're privileged to use His name. As such, we must take it seriously, understanding the power it affords us when we call on that name. His name allows us to perfectly ***activate*** every aspect of our lives.

God's instructions are clear, but we decide not to read and follow them, and then we wonder why our prayers are not being answered. You're living life, things are going well, but are you getting the optimal or maximum benefits from your prayers? You may never have noticed it, but John 14:14 is a repetitive of verse 13. Why did Christ repeat it? Because He knew that some of us would attempt to pray without reading and following His instructions. As such, being the kind of God that He is, He repeated it, hoping that we would catch it the second time. God always has our best interests at heart. We simply need to read and follow His instructions. We have no reason to doubt when praying, God has doubly promised to answer. He said—"*...I will do it.*"

My Prayer

Father, help us to live fuller lives by reading and following Your instructions. In the name of Jesus, we pray. Amen.

What Are Your Thoughts?

What is Your Prayer?

INSTRUCTIONS INCLUDED

Discussion Questions

1 If the instruction is to direct our prayer to Jesus, why are we asking everyone else?

2 When we pray and look for answers, why is it a "privilege to be limited within God's limitless will"?

3 What must we do to ensure we're following all of God's instructions for our prayer lives?

Notes

[1] Watchman Nee, *The Prayer Ministry of the Church* (New York: Christian Fellowship Publishers, 1973), 67.

WEEK 17
A STRAIGHT LINE

*He fulfills the desires of those who fear him;
he hears their cry and saves them.*

—Psalm 145:19 (NIV)

Distance is the extent or amount of space between two things. In the mathematical realm, *distance* is "the numerical descriptions of how far apart objects are." While I'm not the best at it, one of my favorite subjects is math. As I said to my daughter a few days ago while driving her to school, "Math is *clean*." It is either right or wrong. Unlike writing a sentence where everyone has a subjective opinion about your choice of words or structure, math is *clean*; it's either right or wrong.

Here is a math problem for you: given a set of points on a plane, find the shortest line segment formed by any two of these points. Hint: the shortest distance between two points is a straight line. In other words, you can get to your desired destination faster when the path taken is a straight line. I was walking across campus one day, trying to chart a straight path, and the

Holy Spirit said to me: the shortest distance between your desires and fulfillment is sincere prayer. In the spiritual realm you can go from desire to fulfillment faster when the path taken is a straight line to the throne of grace—prayer.

My straight path across campus that afternoon was filled with obstacles—students, buildings, and gates. Bertolt Brecht pointed out, "As regard obstacles, the shortest distance between two points can be a curve."[1] True, but we can avoid having to take curves in our spiritual lives by eliminating the obstacle of *not* fearing God. We must fear Him. Our fear of God is the catalyst for the intensity of our prayers. When we fear God, our desires are fulfilled, prayers are heard, and we are saved. Stick with the straight line—God is ready to hear and answer the prayers of His people.

While the fulfillment of our desires is only a prayer away, God will not slackly fulfill the desires of anyone and everyone. What do you desire? You'll have to tell God; you'll have to pray. Those who fear God don't really have their own desires; they usually pray the desires of God. One of the greatest desires that we can have and pray for is the desire to be saved. Christians who fear God make righteous requests through prayer. As noted in our focus text, these desirers are readily heard, fulfilled, and lead to salvation.

As Christians, we should not be scared of God. Instead, we are to fear him. To fear God is to be in an attitude of reverence, total awe, respect, and worship in all things related to Him, especially prayer. Is your cry for His saving grace and everything that comes with it? Don't be afraid to cry and pray. Tears associated with prayer are usually earnest and sincere. Charles Spurgeon reminds us, "Tears clear the eyes for the sight of God in His grace and make the vision of His favor more precious."[2] Many of us don't like to cry, but tears are necessary sometimes to give us a clearer view of God and His blessings. Tears remove impurities from the eyes.

Unfortunately, for too many of us, things are far apart. There can be tremendous distance between our heart's desires and the fulfillment of those desires. Know, however, that if we fear God and cry out to Him, He will hear our prayers, fulfill our desires, and save us. Avoid the curves; take a straight line directly to the throne of grace. The shortest distance between your desires and fulfillment of those desires is sincere prayer.

My Prayer

Father, as we pray, give us the desires of our heart. Amen.

What Are Your Thoughts?

What is Your Prayer?

Discussion Questions

1. What are some of the obstacles that block our prayers from reaching the throne of grace?

   _____

   _____

   _____

2. Describe how prayer is the shortest line to the throne of grace.

   _____

   _____

   _____

3. What is the relationship between the fear of God and genuine prayer?

   _____

   _____

   _____

Notes

[1] Bertolt Brecht, *AZ Quotes*, *https://www.azquotes.com/quote/572365*.

[2] Charles Spurgeon, *Faith's Checkbook—A Treasury of Daily Devotions*, Oneplace.com, 2020, (*https://www.oneplace.com/ministries/spurgeon-sermons/read/devotionals/faiths-checkbook-ch-spurgeon/faiths-checkbook-august-21-11551929.html*), August 21.

Month 5

Week 18

Two or Three: Families and Prayer

I promise that when any two of you on earth agree about something you are praying for, my Father in heaven will do it for you. Whenever two or three of you come together in my name, I am there with you.

—Matthew 18:19-20 (CEV)

Scripture is clear that some praying ought to be done in the closet and with the door closed. "But thou, when thou prayest, enter into thy closet, and when thou hast shut thy door…" Matthew 6:6 (KJV). It is interesting to note that most closets are small and would not be able to comfortably accommodate two or more individuals. Therefore, without a doubt, we are clearly admonished that some praying must be individual, personal, private.

Conversely, our focus text is pregnant with promises for those of us who come together in His name to pray about some matter. Still, our inability to assemble collectively in prayer prevents us from realizing the blessings of answered prayer and even more important, from experiencing God's presence. Private, personal, or individual prayer, as already noted, has its place, but there is great value when two or three join together in prayer.

Accordingly, biological families must make time to gather and pray for two reasons. First, God stands ready to answer our prayers. The key word in the former sentence is "make." Families are very busy (work, school, church) with good things, but unless we make time for prayer it may not happen. Second, God will dwell among us if we gather in His name. The praying of two or three produces unity that allows us to gather in one accord—in His name. God loves to hang out with Christians who are in agreement.

Stick with me a while longer and extend this text to the church family. When families pray together at home, it has tremendous impact on the church family. It is astonishing to think of the power for life-changing ministry available to us when individual families, who are experiencing answered prayer and God's presence, come together as one—the church.

My Prayer

Father, we know that a threefold cord is not quickly broken; and so, I pray for unity in our families and the church family. Amen.

TWO OR THREE: FAMILIES AND PRAYER

WHAT ARE YOUR THOUGHTS?

WHAT IS YOUR PRAYER?

Discussion Questions

1. How is closet prayer different from church (congregational) praying?

2. How does our lack of congregational prayer prevent us from experiencing God's blessings?

3. What is the relationship between prayer, unity, and God's presence in the church?

Week 19

I've Heard Your Request

To God Abraham said,
"If only you would accept Ishmael!"

—Genesis 17:18 (CEB)

Frequently, because of our lack of faith and our impatience, we attempt to help God out, and we end up sinning. More often than not, our disobedience complicates life. Many of us blame Eve, and some similarly fault Sarah, but the bottom-line is, like many of us, Abraham erred; he sinned. Genesis 16: 1-4 tells us that Sarah gave her handmaid to her husband to be his wife. Abraham slept with Hagar, and she conceived a child—Ishmael.

All of us have conceived and given birth to "Ishmaels" because we choose to do things our way. We would do well to remember that God does not need our help. What He requires is our trust and obedience. Our sins will get us into situations and positions where our only way of escape is prayer. When we sin, most of us continue to walk away from God instead of turning and walking toward Him through prayer. Know, however, that while we're separated from God because of our sins, prayer is the bridge that can void the gap. So, Abraham prayed, "If only you would accept Ishmael!"

Like Abraham, we're concerned about our "Ishmaels." What will happen to all that I've done? What will become of all *my* plans? God will ignore our plans to implement what He has ordained. Our disobedience or alternative planning will never cause God to alter His plans (covenant) to appease us or to save us from public embarrassment. Yet, He will cover us—what grace!

God is now ready, some 25 years later, to confirm His promise, but there is another heir. Some criticize Abraham for praying a selfish prayer, but what parent would not pray the same for his child? I can only imagine that Abraham thought that after 13 years, God was going to remove (kill) Ishmael and replace him with Isaac. While it's hard for us to comprehend, God would have been fair in taking this course of action. His response to Abraham shows, however, that if we pray, He will take our sin-produced mess and restore His order.

Nevertheless, the consequences of our disobedience could hang around as a reminder of our unfaithfulness and impatience. It's been a while, even years, since you made that mistake, and it may appear that God has forgotten or that He has changed His plans. Don't be fooled; what God has ordained will always come to pass. There is no expiration date on the promises of God. When you're reminded of how far you've drifted from God's plans, it's time to pray. Know that God will hear and answer your prayer; He will not adjust His plans but will grant you grace. While Abraham's prayer was not in keeping with God's covenant, it was a sincere prayer from his heart.

God said to Abraham: "No." In other words, this is not the plan I had for you, but I've heard your prayer. We can never dictate to God, especially when we've sinned; yet in prayer we can humbly plead His mercies. Herein is the power of prayer: it allows us to turn our backs on our shortcomings and look to the One who can fix them. We must try to avoid living outside of God's will. However, if it does happen, don't allow anyone to block your clemency. You must pray to the One who established the covenant and ask Him to correct the situation. Know that God will not and does not abandon us—even in our sins.

This is not permission to sin; rather, it is authorization to deal with sin at the spiritual and not the human level. As humans, it's difficult sometimes to comprehend and accept what is happening in the spiritual realm. Prayer (communication with God) is the best way for us to gain an understanding and at some level attain the acceptance for what is happening in the spiritual realm.

While your foolish mistakes will come with consequences, God will hear and answer your prayers. If you've gone against God's will and have allowed anyone (Sarah, Hagar) to interject themselves into your life thereby impeding God's purpose for your life, know that God can and will give you peace. He will not excuse your sin but will provide a sweet level of assurance—"As for Ishmael, I've heard your request. I will bless him" (v. 20).

My Prayer

Father, show us Your grace and let us feel Your mercy. Amen.

What Are Your Thoughts?

What is Your Prayer?

DISCUSSION QUESTIONS

1 Why is prayer so much more necessary when we've conceived and given birth to our Ishmaels?

2 Is praying about the situation after sinning presumptuous?

3 Prayers for forgiveness will not eliminate the consequences, so why pray?

Week 20

The Blessings of Intercessory Prayer

After Job had prayed for his friends, the Lord restored his fortunes and gave him twice as much as he had before.

—Job 42:10 (NIV)

We're told (Romans 8:34) that Christ is at the right hand of God interceding for us. As our example, we must similarly pray for others. We're called throughout Scripture (e.g., James 5:16) to pray for each other. We must mediate, plead, and negotiate with God on behalf of others. When we do, we're engaged in intercessory prayer. As Christians, we often testify about the life-changing power of intercessory prayer. For example, when we intercede for others, they secure employment, they recover from illness, they pass exams, or they accept Christ as Savior.

We infrequently talk, however, about the blessings of intercessory prayer for the intercessor. Yes, blessings await those of us who pray for others. "Unintended Consequences" is a concept found in sociology and other disciplines. The term is used to describe outcomes that are not the ones intended by a purposeful action. In our current context, the intended consequence was Job's obedience. However, Job's ordered prayer for his friends (a purposeful action) resulted in God's restoring his fortunes and doubling it (an unintended consequence).

Is God withholding any blessings from you because you're not praying for others? No guilt intended—just a call for you to reflect on your priorities as they relate to intercessory prayer. If you're honest with yourself, you'll have to admit that you often spend more time praying for yourself than for others. While God does and will answer your prayers for yourself, He takes great pleasure in knowing that you took the time to intercede for others.

God will often place burdens on your hearts to pray for each other and at times will provide specifics—forgiveness, healing, relationships, etc. When you pray for others, He will restore your fortunes and then double them. This restoration, however, does not guarantee financial wealth. Believe it or not, God's fortunes for you includes much more than money. Remember, Job's fortunes included his property as well as his spiritual, emotional, and physical health, family, friends, and reputation.

We can never do anything to gain God's favor; it is a free gift. It is totally up to Him, if, when, and how He decides to bless us. Still, are you waiting on God to do or do even more in your life? Then begin to intercede sincerely for others. Christ is the great intercessor, and we are to follow His example. Focus on pleading for others, and God will focus on you. There are great unanticipated blessings in intercessory prayer. Don't miss out!

My Prayer

As our singular example, Father, I pray that we will take the time to pray for others. Amen.

THE BLESSINGS OF INTERCESSORY PRAYER

WHAT ARE YOUR THOUGHTS?

WHAT IS YOUR PRAYER?

Discussion Questions

1 Why is there so much power in intercessory prayer?

2 Like Job, can we experience unintended blessings by praying for others?

3 What is the relationship between obedience, intercessory prayer, and God's blessings?

Week 21

Get on the Wall

O Jerusalem, I have set intercessors (watchmen) on your walls who shall cry to God all day and all night for the fulfillment of his promises. Take no rest, all you who pray, and give God no rest until he establishes Jerusalem and makes her respected and admired throughout the earth.

—Isaiah 62:6-7 (TLB)

In biblical times cities had huge walls (i.e., the walled city of Jericho), and watchmen stationed on those walls had an extremely critical job. The watchmen were the second line of defense as they were to warn the city of approaching threats. The responsibility of the watchmen was to protect the city from danger. Moreover, the watchmen were held personally responsible for spotting danger and for sounding the alarm. They were the first sight and voice of the city. So important was their role that if they were found sleeping on the job or if they neglected their duties in any other way, they could be put to death.

Our focus text is from The Living Bible and uses the term *intercessors* as a substitute for "watchmen." The use of the term *intercessor* sets in motion a powerful illustration of the significance and outcome of insistent praying. While the city's walls were the first line of defense, the watchmen were the second. Having a walled city where no one is watching only delays pending defeat; it does not prevent it. In other words, accepting Christ as Lord and Savior is our first defense. However, if we're not praying for others and ourselves, it's meaningless. Our defeat is inevitable. The most important responsibility of the watchmen was to watch—hence the job title. As Christians, our chief duty is to pray.

A second and equally important duty of the watchmen was to warn the city of looming danger. The watchmen on duty who perceived approaching danger and failed to sound a proper warning were of no value to the city and its citizens. God, Himself, has appointed us to be intercessors—an assignment that is not voluntary. As such, we're accountable to God for fulfilling our obligation as intercessors. As we stand guard upon the wall, we must *engage* ("cry to God") Him through prayer as we observe a world in danger. The ungodly things of this world must not go unreported; we must sound the alarm. Far too many of us remain prayerless, and the Enemy is allowed to besiege the city—our souls.

Danger has no schedule and makes no appointments; it surfaces when it wants to without much forewarning. Therefore, watchmen were stationed on the walls, day and night. Similarly, as intercessors we are to pray "all day and all night"; intercessors don't clock out. In our secular pursuits, we can be unrelenting. We'll stay up all night to study, wait in line for days to get the new iPhone, or work three jobs to make that purchase. We must also learn to expend ourselves and God in prayer; don't rest. Moreover, notice that He commands us to approach the throne of grace in this manner. We have a directive from God to pray tirelessly. Too often we set unnecessary limits on God and cause a default on ourselves because of our inconsistency in prayer.

At times you don't know what to pray for. No problem. At these times you ought to pray the many promises of God. As an intercessor, you're not crying out (praying) aimlessly. You're petitioning God "for the fulfillment of His promises." What is His promise? God has promised to make us "respected and admired throughout the earth." The only thing God wants for us is the best. So, get on the wall, watchmen, and pray persistently with confidence that God honors His promises. Remember, the city and your life is at stake.

My Prayer

Father help us not to neglect our duty to pray and to warn this world. We know that many souls are at stake. Amen.

What Are Your Thoughts?

What is Your Prayer?

Discussion Questions

1. How is it possible to pray all day and all night?

   _____
   _____
   _____

2. What does it mean to give God no rest in prayer?

   _____
   _____
   _____

3. Can an intercessor's prayer have that much of an impact on God?

   _____
   _____
   _____

Week 22

A Quiet and Peaceful Life

"First of all, then, I urge that petitions, prayers, requests, and thanksgivings be offered to God for all people; for kings and all others who are in authority, that we may live a quiet and peaceful life with all reverence toward God and with proper conduct."

—1 Timothy 2:1-2 (GNT)

Paul in Romans chapter 13 encourages submission to governing authority (vv. 1-7) and love for each other (vv. 8-10). But we're currently living in an age where it's easier, and seemingly abundantly more fruitful to challenge authority and each other rather than submit to and love each other. First, submitting/loving is the right and proper thing to do. And by doing what is right (submitting) and proper (loving), we bring honor and glory to God.

Our focus text takes things a step farther and asks us to also pray for those in authority. God, being the God that He is, attached a promise to this request: the assurance of living a quiet and peaceful life. It's a sad commentary on our existence as humans and the current state of our society when some would outwardly prefer to be at odds with others rather than live a quiet and peaceful life. Many would challenge my observation, but our actions tell the real story. While our social media posts criticizing those in authority and others are likely to go viral on social media, we often don't consider the tremendous consequences of our actions. The instant gratification of gaining likes, re-tweets, and re-posts overshadows the promise found in our focus text.

We live in an ecosystem that's ordered and responsive, i.e., there is always a reaction to our actions. Something or someone is always affected. Because of the complexity of our social networks, we might not perceive the consequences (the reaction) firsthand or immediately. Seeing the consequences may take several years, but at some point, due to the interconnectedness of the system, the correlation is made. This "thing" is as a direct or indirect result of my actions or lack thereof. Similarly, most promises in the Bible are conditional. If you do this, God says, "I'll do this." Specifically, if you pray for "all people" and "kings and all others who are in authority," you'll have "a quiet and peaceful life," i.e., action and reaction.

The action/reaction principle does not limit itself to science or to what some might call karma. This principle is fully functional in the spiritual realm for Christians. Namely, if we pray (our action) for all people and those in authority, we're promised (the reaction) a quiet and peaceful life. The opposite is also true, but most of us reason our way out. Someone is saying, "Don't you know it's hard to pray for someone that I don't want to submit to, that I don't love?" My response: "I know it is, but it's much easier to submit and to love if you're praying for them. Let's lead with prayer."

Paul says to pray for all people. Our love for each other should allow us to offer petitions, prayers, requests, and thanksgiving to God for all people. Many will claim that they do pray for all people. However, when you look closely, you'll realize that we

A QUIET AND PEACEFUL LIFE

can be very selective in who we pray for. Again, the quietness and the peacefulness of your life depends on your ability to pray for "all people"—not just the people you like. We must pray for that neighbor, co-worker, classmate, etc. that we really don't like and are struggling to get along with.

Paul then gets particularly specific. He says, "Pray for 'kings and all others who are in authority.'" In his commentary notes, Matthew Henry writes, "...though the kings at this time were heathens, enemies to Christianity, and persecutors of Christians, yet they must pray for them."[1] Oh boy! Now you're going too far! It's not *me*; it's Paul, and it's biblical! Pray for your supervisor, your pastor, your President, your teacher, your parents, etc.... In other words, stop bashing your supervisor, pastor, President, teacher, or parents and start praying for them.

What is the quality of your life? Have you ever wondered why your life is not as quiet and peaceful as you would like? Think about it... are you really living a quiet and peaceful life? In contemplating these questions, many of us have never connected our negligence to pray for each other and those in authority with our raucous and lawless lives—action and reaction. We have yet to realize the promise of our focus text, but we're not making the connection. The miserable life you're living could be as a direct result of your disregard to first submit to authority, to love each other, and subsequently to pray for them.

Some Christians are posting, protesting, and picketing, but they're not doing it from a position of love and even further not from the perspective of being obedient to God. Accordingly, the lawlessness we're witnessing in our lives and currently in our collective society is a direct result of our prayerlessness. Nevertheless, I'm encouraged by this promise of God outlined for us by Paul: pray for "all people; for kings and all others who are in authority," and you'll "live a quiet and peaceful life." You should trust God to act when you pray. The promise is true; the consequences are real—pray!

My Prayer

Father, help us to be obedient, to pray, and to enjoy a quiet and peaceful life. Amen.

What Are Your Thoughts?

What is Your Prayer?

Discussion Questions

1. Why is it so difficult for us to pray for individuals in authority?

   _____
   _____
   _____

2. How can Christians set an example for the rest of the world by praying for individuals they don't like?

   _____
   _____
   _____

3. Can it really be true, that our current negative situation is due to our prayerlessness?

   _____
   _____
   _____

Notes

[1] Matthew Henry, *Matthew Henry's Commentary on the Whole Bible* (Peabody, Mass.: Hendrickson Publishers, 1991), 2352.

Month 6

Week 23

Thy Will Be Done

He went away again the second time, and prayed, saying, O my Father, if this cup may not pass away from me, except I drink it, thy will be done.

—Matthew 26:42 (KJV)

A few years ago, I sat in a Bible study class and listened to a discussion. The dialogue began as a result of this question: was the plan of salvation as we know it the only plan or was there another plan had Jesus opted out? I'm convinced that there was no other plan. Scripture tells us that the plan of redemption was formed before the foundation of the world (1 Peter 1:20, Revelation 13:8). Upon further reflection, I became curious—not about whether Jesus had a way out, but about the process that allowed Him to follow the plan as designed. In other words, what was it that allowed Him to follow through? Delightfully, I report today that what allowed Jesus to complete the plan of redemption was prayer.

First, notice that Jesus initially recognized His need to pray and for prayer before He verbalized His concerns to anyone

(Matthew 26:36, 38). We must be so in-tune with God that we will sense the need to pray and for prayer before the problem and/or concern materializes. The Lord is trying to direct us toward a higher goal, and we can't see it because we're not praying. Our spiritual antennas are broken or so out of range that we can't recognize our pending danger. We can't sense that the Devil is after us, and so we don't know that there is a need to pray and for prayer.

Second, as Jesus did, it is good to seek and to have the assistance of each other in prayer when we're distressed. Still, when faced with a problem, please be careful who you ask to or take with you to pray (v. 37). Some of our prayers are so weak that they don't get past the ceiling. When you're facing life's most difficult challenges, you want to know that somebody somewhere is watching and praying for and with you. When church folks, however, won't corporate with you in prayer, you have to leave them alone (v. 44). Again, be careful who you ask to or take with you to pray.

Third, don't change or abandon your prayer unless or until God tells you, "I'm not going to answer that prayer." What do you do when you've prayed three times, and God does not answer your prayer? You keep praying. Most of us don't get to the throne of grace because we give up too soon. Jesus prayed three times: "If it is possible…" or "if there is another way." He knew what He had to do, but in His human state, Jesus was having a difficult time. He petitioned His Father for help: "May this cup be taken from me." He quickly follows though by letting His Father know that He would honor His will and that He would be obedient to the original and only plan—"not as I will, but as you will." In other words, "Do what You have to do, and not what I want done."

Finally, realize that submission to God's will does not always eliminate the struggle. Sometimes God will not remove the trial but will give you strength to deal with it. Jesus said, "Rise, let us go! Here comes my betrayer!" (v. 46). When you allow God's will to be done, you'll see the problem (the betrayer) coming, and you'll rise to meet it head-on. You know that when you allow God's will to be done, good things will eventually happen. "Thy will be done" as Jesus prayed is the most difficult prayer to pray. It is a difficult prayer because you're fully relinquishing your position in favor of God's. Conversely, it is the most powerful prayer. Why? Because it leaves you in a position of strength—good things will happen, eventually.

My Prayer

Father, thy will be done. Amen.

What Are Your Thoughts?

What is Your Prayer?

DISCUSSION QUESTIONS

1. What was it about prayer that allowed Jesus to follow through with the plan of redemption?

2. What do we do when we've prayed and prayed, but there's still no answer?

3. Why is "thy will be done" the most difficult prayer?

Week 24

No Glory

I brought glory to you here on earth by completing the work you gave me to do.

—John 17:4 (NLT)

On the night of His betrayal, right before His crucifixion, Jesus prayed to His Father. It is the longest recorded prayer of Jesus. He was exceedingly specific in that prayer: "I have completed the work You gave me to do." Not only had He finished the work, but Jesus was pleased that He had brought glory to God while on earth. In other words, He was humbly proud about what He was able to accomplish.

The latter part of our focus text, "…by completing the work you gave me to do," explains the former portion: "I brought glory to you here on earth." As we look around this earth, Christians are not finishing the work; consequently, God's name now gets limited to no glory. God is getting no glory on earth because we're not engaged in "the work." Too many of our churches and individuals alike are not well-appointed and are distracted from the work.

What work? As He prayed, Christ had nothing more to do, but die. Christ came to bring deliverance. He did His part, and in so doing, brought glory to God. Like Christ, we also have a work to complete. The church, with the assistance of the Holy Spirit, must now perfect the work He commenced. Our task is an end-time commission to tell others about Christ. If done properly, we too will bring glory to God. So, here is the essential question: how can we finish the work and bring God the glory He deserves? The answer: our churches must become houses of prayer!

Note, intense prayer throughout His earthly ministry allowed Christ to finish the work and to say with confidence, "I brought glory to you here on earth...." Prayer coupled with work equals glory. When we're not praying (and our churches are not houses of prayer), we're not equipped and engaged with the spiritual affluence to complete the work. Subsequently, no meaningful work is accomplished, and God gets no glory. No prayer, no work, no glory.

In closing, notice that Christ's ultimate purpose for presenting this report of His achievements was to re-claim His former status—divine glory (John 17:5). In other words, "Father, bring me into the glory we once shared before the world began." If this is your first time reading this passage, you must admit, it sounds somewhat self-centered. Nothing is selfish, however, about wanting to be in God's presence.

When your time comes to report, will you be able to humbly, yet proudly, say you've worked as needed and that His name has been glorified? Through your sincere prayer, God will equip you to finish His work and bring Him glory. Aren't you tired of the separation? Aren't you ready to go home? If you're ready to go home or ready to re-claim your rightful position as son or daughter of God, start praying.

My Prayer

Father, I pray that through the power of the Holy Spirit, we will work to bring You glory. Amen.

What Are Your Thoughts?

What is Your Prayer?

Discussion Questions

1 "No prayer, no work, no glory." As such, what must we do to bring God His glory?

2 What is the impact of a praying church on evangelism?

3 Why are so many churches distracted from prayer and finishing the work?

Week 25

After the High

*Before daybreak the next morning, Jesus got up
and went out to an isolated place to pray.*

—Mark 1:35 (NLT)

On December 5, 2015, with the assistance of family and the best group of friends in the world, I was able to launch my new book. It was a great evening as my church family, colleagues, and visitors came out to support the launch. After the event, I stayed up until 2:00 a.m. the next morning, talking with my wife and mother-in-law about the experience. I was up again early that morning for a 9:00 a.m. meeting at church.

After I returned home later that evening, my mother-in-law asked, "Are you still on a high from the event last night?" As I reflect on our exchange, I cannot recall my exact response because I was in awe at what God had just done. No, not in the success of the book launch and reception, but what He had shared with me prior to the launch...

Earlier in the week leading up to the event, God directed me to our focus text. I took a few notes and decided that, at some point, I would use it for one of these essays. I titled it *After the High*. My mother-in-law's question was a reminder that I needed to manage my emotions, come down from my high, and prayerfully prepare myself for the work ahead.

Success can produce a great natural high—no artificial stimulants required. Nevertheless, after you've done well (ministered), you've got to come down and get on your knees. You've got to make time for prayer. In the background of the focus text, Jesus had amazed, astonished, and impressed the crowd. He had performed many miracles that had elevated His reputation (vv. 23-34). His fame was now spreading throughout the region and beyond. So, what did He do next? He prayed.

When our "fame" spreads and we're on our spiritual high, too many of us neglect the source of our strength; we abandon or become reckless with prayer. This is not the time to get so caught up in ministry that we squander or short-circuit the source of our power for ministry. Conversely, this is the time when we should be praying for (1) humility (2) more opportunities for ministry (3) the desire to remain focused in ministry (4) more power for ministry, and (5) success in future ministry.

Remember that ministry (doing good) is honorable, but it should never distract us from connecting with God. Too often, however, it does. What good are you and the ministry if there is no spiritual power to transform lives? A prayerless ministry is simply a nice program or activity. Some of us get caught up in ministry because it makes us feel good; we're riding the spiritual high. It's a good high and a wonderful ride, but we need to be very careful. We could end up leading others to Christ while we ourselves gradually drift away from Him because of our prayerlessness.

Noise and people—crowds—usually accompany spiritual highs. Success often leads to crowds and sometimes the crowd can be distracting. So, after the high, you've got to get up early, find a quiet place, and pray. You've got to go early to connect with

Christ while others are asleep. Similarly, you'll need to find a quiet place where you can block out the distractions of the crowd. Jesus left His disciples behind; we too will have to leave family, friends, and associates behind. All conversations with God are not and should not be public. Just as we will sometimes speak with others in private, away from intrusions, it should be no different in our conversations with God.

Finally, we must not allow our spiritual highs to distract us from effective ministry in the future. We have to be prayed-up to move on to the next assignment and to remember why we've been called. If we don't make time to pray, spiritual highs can rob us of our focus and distract us from future assignments and success. With renewed power gained through prayer, Christ said, "We must go on to other towns as well, and I will preach to them too. That is why I came" (v. 38). When we come down and get down, we'll have power to sustain our focus and continue the work.

My Prayer

Father, give us success in ministry and the wisdom to pray despite our success. Amen.

What Are Your Thoughts?

What is Your Prayer?

Discussion Questions

1 Why is it so difficult for us to pray after ministry highs?

2 Why is it necessary to get away from all distractions and pray?

3 What's the significance of prayer as it relates to ministry success, now and in the future?

Week 26

What Are You Hungry for?

> *"Jesus replied, "I am the bread of life.*
> *Whoever comes to me will never be hungry again.*
> *Whoever believes in me will never be thirsty."*
>
> —John 6:35 (NLT)

Most of us at some point, whether as a child or an adult, have made the statement, "I'm hungry." When you find yourself in this situation and recognize your need for food, the essential question is, "What are you hungry for?" This is a common retort by many parents, wives, or friends when someone says, "I'm hungry." "What are you hungry for?" is not a rhetorical question. It's a question that necessitates a response if you intend to address your hunger.

Bread, a common food item to placate hunger, has been around for centuries. Experts believe the first grinding stone used to grind wheat was invented by the Egyptians circa 8000 B.C.[1] Many who are dieting will stay away from bread—too many carbs. Still, bread remains a source of complex carbohydrates, phytochemicals and antioxidants, and fiber.[2] In other words, wheat is a source of energy, whole grain, and promotes good digestive health.

In a general sense, to be hungry is to have a strong desire or craving for something. In the context of our focus Scripture, hunger is a feeling of discomfort or weakness caused by a lack of food, coupled with the desire to eat. This desire to eat must be fulfilled in order to alleviate the discomfort and/or weakness associated with hunger. If this desire for food (to eat) is met, the creature can usually survive. This desire going unmet typically results in death. Sometimes the death is very slow and painful as the creature starves to death.

While many may not purchase and eat bread because they're trying to limit their carb intake, for many households, bread is a staple. Likewise, bread can also be found throughout Scripture—nourishing, sustaining, and satisfying the people:

- We need bread every day to be nourished. "Give us this day our daily bread (Matthew 6:11).
- Bread can also sustain the individual. Bread (manna) was provided to sustain the Israelites in the wilderness (Exodus 16:35).
- If we have bread, we'll be satisfied and in need of nothing as our "bread and water shall be sure" (Isaiah 33:16).

What is this bread that nourishes, sustains, and satisfies? It is Christ, who says, "I am the bread of life." What bread is to our physical bodies, Christ is to the spiritual body. Bread is only bread until it is used. The point when the bread is eaten and digested is when it begins to nourish, sustain, and satisfy the body. The same is true with Christ (our spiritual bread). Until we accept Him as Lord and Savior, we remain starved Christians—uncomfortable and weak. We're not nourished, sustained, and/or satisfied.

We're experiencing spiritual discomfort and weakness, but we must have a desire to eat. As such, we must pray for bread—Christ.

We must pray for Christ, the bread of life. Spiritually, we're starving to death, and we don't even know we're dying a slow and painful death. Too many of us are desirous of things that will never appease our spiritual appetites. We keep eating and eating all the bread that the world has to offer, but still we're not nourished, sustained, or satisfied. Accordingly, we must pray and ask Christ to provide our daily bread—bread that will nourish and sustain, bread that will satisfy.

When it comes to spiritual hunger, the question, "What are you hungry for?" is similarly not a rhetorical question. Bread is life; bread is Christ. Bread is available to you; respond to the call and eat. If you maintain your connection with Christ through prayer, you'll never again experience the spiritual discomfort or weakness associated with spiritual hunger. His promise to you is clear and certain: "whoever comes to me will never be hungry again." Christ is not only asking you "What are you hungry for?" He's also providing the remedy: "I am the bread of life."

My Prayer

Father, fill us. Amen.

What Are Your Thoughts?

What is Your Prayer?

Discussion Questions

1 Is it enough only to pray for our daily bread?

2 What must our prayer be, knowing that Jesus has promised to provide bread?

3 Spiritual hunger is real in our society today. How do we prayerfully feed others?

Notes

[1] Elizabeth Raum, *The Story Behind Bread* (Chicago: Heinemann-Raintree Library, 2009), 28.

[2] North American Millers' Association, *Six Things Everyone Should Know About Wheat in Our Diet* (https://www.namamillers.org/education/six-things-everyone-should-know-about-wheat-in-our-diet/)

MONTH 7

Week 27

You Gotta Sing!

How shall we sing the Lord's song in a strange land?

—Psalm 137:4 (KJV)

As a child growing up, I would listen to my grandmother sing hymns as she worked around the house. Years later, I observed the same mode of expression from my mother. I can recall watching and listening to her sing as she washed dishes, cooked, or cleaned. Guess what? As an adult, I now find myself singing as I move and work around the house. Why do we sing? Well, we're actually praying—singing is a form of praying. The singing of songs is an expression of our deepest human emotions to Christ.

There are times when the only thing we can do is sing. We sing happy songs; we sing sad songs. Whatever the unspeakable sentiment, we sing. Sometimes you just gotta sing. While I cannot recall the specific hymns or songs that my grandmother and mother sung, I now know that their singing was a form of praying. As I reflect upon my selection of songs, I can clearly identify those times when I have sung praises (prayers of thanksgiving) to

God and those times when I have sung (prayers for intervention) to Him in anguish.

When we're out of our comfort zone, too many of us hang up our harps (v. 2)—our instrument of prayer and praise. We sit down crying (v. 1) with our harps hung up, and we do nothing spiritually. Why is it that in our most trying times, we're prayerless? Why is it that our harps are hung, and the melody goes silent? The captors in this Psalm taunted the Israelites to sing: "Sing us one of the songs of Zion" (v. 3). I know it's hard. Don't get me wrong, I understand. Failing a test is failing a test, a court date is a court date, a cancer diagnosis is a cancer diagnosis, captivity is captivity, but you gotta sing (pray).

Like the captors, Satan will taunt us through the complexities of this life. He will mock us to sing when our only alternative seems to be hopelessness. And so we ask, "How shall we sing the Lord's song in a strange land?" (v. 4). Accordingly, we don't sing, we don't pray, we don't praise. At these precise moments, however, we need to be at our highest spiritual level. This is the instance when we most need to represent Christ, and in so doing, we'll be a witness for Him and will correspondingly uncover inner peace.

While captives in this foreign world, you gotta sing. You'd do well to remember that singing is not only a form of praying, it is also a form of witnessing. As noted above, someone is always listening. What better place to sing the Lord's song than in a place where they need to hear it the most? When the request comes, and it will, strange land thou it may be, you gotta sing—pray.

My Prayer

I pray, Father, that You will restore our joy and allow us to honor you with singing. Amen.

What Are Your Thoughts?

What is Your Prayer?

Discussion Questions

1. Why is it that in our most trying times, we're prayerless?

2. Why is it important for us to sing when we cannot find the words to pray?

3. How does maintaining a relationship with Christ through prayer allow us to sing?

Week 28
Show Me Your Glory

*"Then Moses said, "I pray that you will
let me see you in all of your glory."*

—Exodus 33:18 (CEV)

Sometimes in business and/or personally, we meet someone via telephone, e-mail, or now social media. These faceless interactions can go on for weeks, months, or sometimes years. At some point, however, there is a desire by one or both individuals for more; they wish to see each other. I can recall working for a company in New York City that had offices in Connecticut. I would speak to two individuals from the Connecticut payroll office at least twice each day. While there was understandably some desire to meet, to this day we've never met in-person. I've never seen them face-to-face. Similarly, some may recall being set-up for a blind date and having those initial conversations by phone or e-mail, yet longing to finally see the other person face-to-face.

Moses had many intimate conversations with God. He cultivated a prayer life that allowed Him to be a mighty intercessor for

Israel. When God is answering your prayers, it gives you boldness to keep asking. Ultimately, you'll get to the point when you pray that big prayer: "...let me see you in all of your glory." Such boldness is only developed, however, in prior praying. If you're not praying and have never known God to answer your prayers, it is difficult; some would even say presumptuous to approach Him with such boldness as Moses did. Moses was incessantly talking with God, but now he wanted more; he wanted to see Him.

Upon further analysis, his was not an unusual request. How many of us would carry on a conversation with someone and not at some point want to see the person's face? As previously noted, we can talk and talk with each other, but at some point, I want to see your face. Furthermore, Moses had developed a relationship with God where he felt comfortable making such a bold request. Like Moses, as Christians, we cry out to God for a variety of things. We have a lot of needs and so we pray. I'm so glad to know that the more we ask, the more God provides. However, we must get to "that" point where the asking is not so much for things as it is for the One who provides the things.

As true Christians, we must eventually come to the clear spiritual understanding that if I get the Provider, by default I'll also get my heart's desires. We cannot be satisfied to matriculate this earthly life without an intimate relationship and vision of God. Oswald Chambers notes, "It is a bad thing to be satisfied spiritually."[1] Too many of us are satisfied when we should be asking for more: "...let me see you in all of your glory." In our human state, many of us would question Moses' request. "How can you be in such intimate fellowship with God and still be so selfish to ask for more?" Yet God never interprets a desire for more of Him as selfishness. "Show me your glory" is a request that God is always eager to answer.

Like Moses, you want more. You're ready to go deeper and higher in your prayer life, but you're thinking to yourself, *"I can't see God's glory and live"* (v. 20). Don't you worry about that. You make the request and allow God to work out the details. God says, "You want to see My glory, you can't. But I'll show you My goodness." Asking more from God and getting less is always more than what the world has to offer. God's goodness (His back) is sufficient for us. God is willing to allow us to see His back (v. 23), but even that will never happen until we pray to see His face. Oh, what would it be like if instead of praying for things, we prayed to see God in all His glory?

My Prayer

Father, we pray not for things, but for a glimpse of the Provider. Let us see You in all of Your glory. Amen.

What Are Your Thoughts?

What is Your Prayer?

Discussion Questions

1. Do we ever pray to see God in all of His glory?

2. Why is it important for us to have a prior relationship with God before we pray such bold prayers?

3. How do we get to the point where the praying is not for things, but for the One who provides the things?

Notes

[1] Oswald Chambers, *My Utmost for His Highest Daily Devotional* (*https://utmosthighest.blogspot.com/2017/05/my-utmost-passion-of-patience.html*), May 1, 2017.

Week 29

In That Moment

Then the king said unto me, For what dost thou make request? So I prayed to the God of heaven.

—Nehemiah 2:4 (KJV)

Life is complex and difficult. It was for Nehemiah, and it's the same for us today. As Christians, we've been taught from an early age to pray when confronted by difficulty, danger, or disaster. Accordingly, when our walls are broken and our gates are burnt (Nehemiah 1:3), we follow the example of Christ and others. We do what we've been taught; we retreat to fast and pray (v. 4). Following these examples is wise; however, there are times when prayer is needed immediately—in the moment. There's no time to retreat.

No one needs to know you're praying or what you've prayed. In our focus text, we're not told what Nehemiah prayed. We're simply told that he prayed and continued his conversation with the king. Like Nehemiah, at some point you'll find yourself in a perplexing situation, and all you'll be able to say is: "Lord, save me" (Matthew 14:30). You'll have only a moment to pray. As with Nehemiah, the challenge will not always afford us the regular luxuries of prayer:

- No fasting
- No closed eyes
- No kneeling
- No crying
- No confession of sin
- No reading of promises
- No quite place
- No prayer partner
- No prayer request
- No flowery language

I did not fast. I did not kneel. I did not confess my sins. Did He hear that prayer? Here is the essential question: should we ever find ourselves in this situation, does God hear "moment prayers"? The simple answer is yes, He does. Still, we would do well to consider who is praying and to Whom. In our focus text, we find Nehemiah (the *who*) is praying, and he prayed to the God of heaven (the *whom*).

This was not the first time that Nehemiah prayed. Herbert Lockyer notes, "...prayer was the maintained attitude and constant habit of Nehemiah. He prayed all the time, all the way through and about everything."[1] Nehemiah's prior prayer relationship is well documented. "...I sat down and wept, and mourned certain days, and fasted, and prayed before the God of heaven" (Nehemiah 1:4). Our prior prayer relationship with God will permit us to approach Him in this manner, in the moment, without it being disrespectful. While God can and will respond to any type of prayer, I encourage you not to let your current perplexity be your first interaction with Him.

Nehemiah stated clearly to whom he prayed—"the God of heaven." Similarly, Peter cried out, "Lord, save me." These instantaneous prayers were honored because of whom they prayed to—"I will do whatever you ask in my name" (John 14:13). Calling on the name of God is always a meaningful endeavor. That moment of prayer is not wasted. Whenever we petition God, we can be certain that He will hear. When the King of kings says, "…for what dost thou make request?" in that moment pray; He will hear and answer you.

My Prayer

I pray, Lord, that we will solicit the God of heaven in that moment. Amen.

WHAT ARE YOUR THOUGHTS?

WHAT IS YOUR PRAYER?

Discussion Questions

1 Why is it good to have had a prior prayer relationship with God before praying "in-the-moment" prayers?

2 What do you do when circumstance will not allow for prayer decorum because prayer is needed right away?

3 What happens to our prayers when we're unable to engage in the luxuries of prayer?

Notes

[1] Herbert Lockyer, *All the Prayers of the Bible* (Grand Rapids: Zondervan, 1959), 90.

Week 30

Tear Up the Roof

They couldn't bring him to Jesus because of the crowd, so they dug a hole through the roof above his head. Then they lowered the man on his mat, right down in front of Jesus.

—Mark 2:4 (NLT)

I've said it in earlier writings and you've heard it many times before that prayer is communication with God. Generally, when we say prayer is communication, more often than not, we mean uttering words. However, just as we have non-verbal communication, we also have non-verbal prayers. Yes, believe it or not, we can actually pray without ever using any words. As we're able to pray with words, in much the same way we can pray with our actions. I like to call it "action prayer"—it takes prayer to a different level.

Our focus text notes, "They couldn't bring him to Jesus because of the crowd." Sometimes, sorrow, pain, fear, confusion, anger, sin, etc. will block our path to Jesus. At some point in your prayer life, you'll have to do whatever is necessary to get to Jesus—even tear up the roof to get to Him. Essentially, you'll have to take action. What's the old saying? "Actions speak louder than words." If you've never had the experience, the day will come when you'll attempt to pray and you're unable to verbally articulate your desires. During those times, know that you can communicate your desires to God without speaking—take action.

At times we may not have the words, but our actions will express our desire. Again, our prayers will not be audible but will take the form of action. This type of praying, however, could get you into trouble. Allow me to share the danger associated with action prayer. Action prayer may seem presumptuous to onlookers. All others see is your actions, while the expression of desire is hidden from their sight. In the human realm, you just showed up without representation for the court date. But in the spiritual realm, your effort was equivalent to a prayer. As such, we should be helpful and supportive when we see others taking action.

Here is the action prayer in our focus text: they carried him to the house, took him up to the roof, dug a hole in the roof, and lowered him to Jesus. The voice of this paralyzed man is silent as is the voice of his friends. All we see is action. I encourage you never to allow the Devil to keep you boxed in when pain and fear is too much for words—take action. Don't sit in silence and suffer; do something to get to Jesus. This is amazing! Notice that it was his friends who brought him to the house, carried him to the roof, dug the hole in the roof, and lowered him in front of Jesus.

"Four men arrived carrying him" is akin to intercessory prayer. If you can't do it yourself, be careful to surround yourself with Christians who can get you to Jesus. Good Christian friends will notice when you're unable to pray and will help you move into action prayer. Some of us, however, start praying for others and then when it gets too difficult because of the "crowd," we give up. No, don't stop; if necessary, tear up the roof to get to Jesus. At some point, collectively, we'll have to take action to get our prayers answered. When your verbal prayer can't get others in front of Jesus, try action prayer.

The deeds on the part of this man's friends were to secure healing; it was action prayer. Their actions were very calculated. They were not coming thinking that *maybe* he will be healed. Their determination to get in front of Jesus was a clear expression of their expectation. It was a manifestation of their faith. If you look at Mark 1, you will see that Jesus was on a miracle tour. He healed many people who were sick with various diseases, and He cast out many demons. Namely, He cast out an evil spirit, healed Simon's mother-in-law, and healed a man with leprosy. They knew what Jesus had done and what He could do, and so they came resolute to do whatever was necessary to get to Jesus.

Action prayer is taking prayer to a different level because it involves persistent faith. Too often you have unmet desires, but you remain silent. Neither do you take any action. Don't sit around complaining and upset about what you don't have when Jesus is in the house. Do whatever is necessary to get into the house. Actions do speak louder than words. God wants to see willingness on your part for an answer, and He will respond. When you move, He'll move. Sometimes you'll come asking for physical healing, and you'll leave with spiritual healing as well (Mark 2:5).

My Prayer

Father, You're in the house; help us to do whatever is necessary to move toward You. Amen.

What Are Your Thoughts?

What is Your Prayer?

Discussion Questions

1 Is it presumptuous for Christians to engage in action prayer?

2 What role must faith play in action prayer?

3 Why are so many Christians suffering when Jesus is in the house, prepared to answer our prayers?

Week 31

Sweet-Smelling Incense

"Let my prayer be set forth before thee as incense; and the lifting up of my hands as the evening sacrifice."

—Psalm 141:2 (KJV)

David, the author of Psalm 141, is in distress. He needs help, so he cries out to God for guidance and protection. When in distress like David, we must cry out to God for His guidance and protection; we must pray. It is wise to seek God's aid; however, our asking for His assistance must be acceptable to Him. In asking for assistance out of our distress, the approach of the one making the request must be pleasing to the one able to deliver relief. In other words, if you're in trouble and need my help, you have to ask nicely. I must be engaged and motivated to help you.

Asking for assistance from God is no different. We cannot and should not expect help from God if we continue to be offensive to Him. Too many of our prayers are offensive to God. Accordingly, He rejects our prayers because they are not like sweet-smelling incense. This is why David in his distress pleaded with God: "Let my prayer be set forth before thee as incense…" Are your prayers offensive to God? Will your prayers be heard and answered? Are your prayers assured of divine acceptance? These are weighty questions that will keep any Christian up at night.

Here is some guidance. According to our focus text, acceptable asking (prayer) is like incense—non-offensive to God. Following are three specific details about incense associated with the sanctuary service that are instructive for our prayer lives.

- ***First, Moses was instructed to use specific spices and specific amounts of each spice*** (Exodus 30:34). For our prayers to be acceptable as incense, we must be specific in our praying. Too often our prayers are too general and uninformed.
- ***Second, the incense was to be pure and holy, reserved for the Lord, and they were instructed to treat it as holy*** (Exodus 30:35-37). For our prayers to be acceptable as incense, we must acknowledge the sacredness of praying. Remember, we're talking to the King of kings.
- ***Third, Aaron was to burn incense every morning and every evening; it was perpetual incense before the Lord*** (Exodus 30:7-8). For our prayers to be acceptable as incense, we must engage in persistent praying. We can never get weary of praying.

The vapors of these specific holy spices burned perpetually were intended to reach God. This was why David begged God to let his prayers be set forth before Him as incense. In his distress, he wanted his prayers to reach God. Many of our prayers, however, never reach its intended target; they never get past the ceiling. They never ascend upward as sweet-smelling incense. Rarely do our prayers fill God's throne room with anything pleasant. The lack of specificity, purity, and determination render many of our prayers offensive to God.

Notice that incense plus fire produced a most sweet aroma. Incense (your prayers) without fire (the Holy Spirit) is useless; it has no life-changing value. However, the combination of these two elements (incense and fire) will yield a most valuable outcome—something sweet and pleasant in your life. When David requested that his prayer would go up to God as incense, he was simply saying: "Lord, I'm praying this specific prayer. I treasure this practice as pure and holy, knowing that it must be perpetual. I pray that it is not offensive to You." There are many theories as to why incense was used in the sanctuary. Whatever your belief, know that it was clearly a symbol of prayer (Revelation 5:8).

My Prayer

King of kings, may our prayers reach Your throne of grace as sweet-smelling incense. Amen.

What Are Your Thoughts?

What is Your Prayer?

Discussion Questions

1 Why are we so challenged when it comes to praying specific prayers?

2 What happened that we no longer see prayer as sacred?

3 What does it mean to engage in persistent praying?

MONTH 8

Week 32

Praying for a Second Chance

*From deep inside the fish Jonah
prayed to the LORD his God:*

—Jonah 2:1 (GNT)

It's Sunday afternoon, and you're on the basketball court. You told all your friends that you had a new spectacular dunk. Everyone is now gathered on the court as they await your dunk. You position yourself, dribble the basketball, take off into the air, but you miss the dunk. What do you say? "Give me another chance!" It's game night again. You team is behind by five points. If you answer this final question correctly, your team wins, and you'll have bragging rights until the next game night. You hear the question, ponder all the options, and respond—C. The answer, however, is D. What do you say? "Give me another chance!"

You've messed up over and over again. You're crying out, "Give me another chance!" But no one seems to be listening. What if God decided to give you a second chance? Here, however, is the more meaningful question: what are you going to do with your second chance? As you consider these questions, allow me to share three remarkable points about second chances that will blow your mind and set you up for future victory. The narrative of Jonah is familiar to most Christians, yet they're so much more to uncover.

First, second chances are necessary because of our disobedience. In verses 1-3 of Jonah chapter 1, we read that he was sent to preach to the city of Nineveh. Jonah, however, paid his fare and boarded a ship going to Tarshish. If you looked at a map, you'll see that Tarshish is in the opposite direction. Many of us are like Jonah. God is calling us in one direction, and we find ourselves paying a great cost to go in the opposite direction—paying to disobey. Why? Because we're trying our best to get away from God and what He's called us to do.

The reason many individuals need a second chance is because they're going in the wrong direction. You're not alone, however. You're like Jonah, Saul, Solomon, David, Abraham, Elijah, Jacob, Peter, and Judas. Second chances are designed for individuals like you and me who are disobedient. Yes, know without a doubt that second chances are necessary because of your disobedience, but be assured today that God wants to give you a second chance.

Second, there's a process to second chances, and it's not easy. In verses 4-17 of Jonah chapter 1, we read of the storm sent by God and the process that Jonah had to go through to get his second chance. Many of us who are disobedient to God—heading in the opposite direction—will find ourselves in a storm. While in the storm, we'll be blamed by everyone around us for being the one to cause the storm. Eventually, they'll abandon us by tossing us overboard. While languishing in the sea of life without any hope of survival, we'll be swallowed up and find ourselves in the belly of the whale. Some of us will spend days, others years, in the belly of the whale where it's dark, wet, messy, slimy, and there's vomit.

Know, however, that the trouble you're experiencing is pushing you toward your second chance. The storms you're experiencing right now are pushing you toward your second chance. When storms come, they move things. When the hurricane, tornado, blizzard, cyclone, or tsunamis come, they move things. God is moving you through to your second chance. God has to get you there, and He'll do whatever is necessary to make it happen. Most of us want a second chance, but we don't want to go through the process. You may not like or agree with the process, but you're getting a second chance.

Third, second chances are not about you but are for God's glory. In verses 1-10 of Jonah chapter 3, we read of Jonah's second chance and the amazing results. Given his second chance, Jonah obeyed God and went to Nineveh. The people heard the message, repented, God changed His mind, and 120,000+ individuals were saved. Second chances are for the honor and glory of God. When Jonah got his second chance, he brought honor and glory to the name of God.

When you get your second chance, are you going to bring honor and glory to God? A second chance is not a right but a gift. Second chances were part of God's original strategic masterplan. So now you're asking: "How do I get to my second chance?" Prayer is the key to your second chance. From deep inside the fish, Jonah prayed to the Lord his God (Jonah 2:1, GNT). Most of us will make the promise to pray when we get out of the belly of the whale. "I'm going to pray when this is all over." No, like Jonah, you'll have to cry out to God from the belly of the whale for your second chance.

"Give me another chance!" What if God decided to give you a second chance? While you're praying and waiting for your second change, keep this in mind. If you get your second chance and God gets no glory, then you've wasted your second chance. And so, the consequential question is this: "What are you going to do with your second chance?"

My Prayer

Father, may we take advantage of our second chance and bring honor and glory to Your name. Amen.

What Are Your Thoughts?

What is Your Prayer?

Discussion Questions

1. Is God obligated to give us a second chance when we pray?

2. If we've prayed for a second chance, why do we still go through the process?

3. After praying and getting a second chance, what must be our response to God?

Week 33

You Have Not

You want things, but you cannot have them, so you are ready to kill; you strongly desire things, but you cannot get them, so you quarrel and fight. You do not have what you want because you do not ask God for it. And when you ask, you do not receive it, because your motives are bad; you ask for things to use for your own pleasures.

—James 4:2-3 (GNT)

Every year happy Thanksgiving celebrations end with quarrels, fights, and/or someone being killed inside a retail store or its parking lot. Individuals are quarreling, fighting, and are willing to kill each other for a position in line, a shopping cart, and a parking space. Why? Because these shoppers are after things—cloths, electronics, toys, and games. They so desire these things, some will quarrel, fight, and even kill to get them. Some of you are saying, "This is why I avoid the stores on Black Friday. I shop online—Cyber Monday." But you're still after things.

Similarly, quarreling, fighting, and killing to realize the American dream is real. Because of globalization and mind-blowing technology, individuals from around the world are mindful of the things they want and the things they strongly desire before they even reach the shores of the United States. Upon arrival, they join with the rest of us in pursuit of things. Again, some of you are saying, "I'm not quarreling, fighting, and killing anyone to achieve my American dream. I'm just working hard." You may not want to admit it, but the disagreements in your homes and your perpetual stress suggests that you are quarreling, fighting, and killing yourself to get the things you want—the things you so strongly desire.

Whether we're in the store, online, or trying to achieve the American dream, James says, we want things; we strongly desire these things. Consequently, some of us will quarrel, fight, and even kill to get them. The real reason some of us don't have is because we're not asking God; we're not praying. And when some of us ask Him, we're asking for the wrong reason—our own pleasure. Our focus text describes two groups of church members—oh boy! Some individuals are willing to quarrel, fight, and kill to get the things they want, but they will not pray. Others are praying but with the wrong motives. Which group are you in?

Are you part of the first group making the effort to go it alone, attempting to get the things you desire in life by any means necessary—but without prayer? James lets us know that we don't have what we want because we're not asking God for it. I know of only one way to ask God, and that is to pray. Stop all the quarreling and fighting. Stop killing yourself and others to get the things of this world—just ask God. God grants us life, strength, vision, intelligence, and opportunity. As such, getting "things" is a blessing from God—one that He's willing to grant if we ask—if we pray.

Someone is saying, "I'm asking—I'm praying. I'm not the one quarreling, fighting, or killing, but I'm still not experiencing God's blessings." Let me suggest that you check yourself. This is about your unwillingness to deny yourself and not about God's reluctance to give. Yes, you're praying, but how are you praying? When we pray with the right motives, we surrender our wants, allowing God to bless us with what we need. God does not mind giving you things for your pleasure. What He prefers, however, is that you pursue the pleasure of others while He seeks your pleasure. Isn't that a good deal?

In other words, when you're blessed and you honor God by sowing into the lives of others, you'll continue to get whatever you pray for. You'll get the things you want, the things you desire, and the things you need. These things are for His glory—not your own pleasure. If it brings Him praise and by default it's also pleasurable to you, great! But please don't expect the pleasures of this life when there is no glory in it for God.

Know that there is nothing wrong with a Christian who wants or strongly desires "things." The problem is more so with the Christian who wants things that are outside of God's will for his/her life. Knowing that they cannot, in good conscious, pray for those things, they do whatever (quarrel, fight, and kill) is necessary to get those things. Furthermore, the problem is with a Christian who prays for things within God's will, but with a wrong motive—self-interest. God will never answer a prayer that will not bring Him praise, honor, and glory. God will never answer any prayer that satisfies my own desires while He is marginalized.

My Prayer

Father, give us the desires of our hearts. But most of all, give us a desire for the pleasure of knowing You. Amen.

What Are Your Thoughts?

What is Your Prayer?

Discussion Questions

1 Why is it better to pray and not quarrel, fight, and kill for things?

2 What must be our motive when we pray for things?

3 God will not answer a prayer that will not bring Him glory. Why?

Week 34

Start Praying!

The Lord said, "I was ready to answer my people's prayers, but they did not pray. I was ready for them to find me, but they did not even try. The nation did not pray to me, even though I was always ready to answer, 'Here I am; I will help you.'"

—Isaiah 65:1 (GNT)

Sometimes I remain overtly silent on some issues for fear of starting avoidable disagreements. My training as a sociologist and researcher forces me to look much deeper at problems. While most individuals may look at what's apparent, I see the obvious as only a symptom of more significant concerns. As such, in discussions, I will compel the person to look beyond the surface for the true cause. What's the source? One of my sayings, "There is always an explanation" often starts the disagreements. To maintain peace, I'll remain quiet and prayerfully observe.

In my quiet moments, I've observed over the last several years that we've been dealing with some very weighty matters—the definition of marriage, impeachment, pending elections, #MeToo, policing, terrorism, LGBT, COVID-19, etc. Hot stuff! Most of us have strong opinions about all of these subjects. My purpose is not to offer my opinion but to suggest a cause and to offer a solution. Finding the root cause often leads to a viable solution. If you're dealing with a health issue, you can get all your friends' opinions, and you can Google all night. The most viable solutions, however, will not surface until you visit your doctor and seek a professional diagnosis.

Our focus text hits the nail on the head. The Great Physician presents His diagnosis. He says, "I was ready to answer my people's prayers, but they did not pray. I was ready for them to find me, but they did not even try. The nation did not pray to me, even though I was always ready to answer, 'Here I am; I will help you.'" In summary, here is His diagnosis: the root cause of the problems we're dealing with as a nation and as a global community is prayerlessness. There is no need for a second opinion. The suggested solution is prayer. God is ready to help if we would seek His face and pray. Start praying!

While we're living in the last days and know that these troubles will arise (see Matthew 24:4-12), God nevertheless stands ready to provide answers to a praying church. But we're not praying. He additionally notes, "And this gospel of the kingdom shall be preached in all the world for a witness unto all nations; and then shall the end come" (v. 14). Those Christians who believe in prophecy love to quote this passage as support for their enthusiastic efforts to reach the world. And since we're rightfully concerned about marriage, terrorism, and COVID-19, we sound the warning. There is absolutely no way, however, for the gospel to reach this world—ushering in His second coming—if we're not praying. Start praying!

God declares, "I was ready for them to find me, but they did not even try." In all that we're doing as the Christian church, are we really trying to help others find Christ? Are we really busying ourselves to give them very opportunity to repent? God has appointed us to be a stabilizing force of truth in a world spiraling out of control. For too many Christians, however, our response to these troubling current issues has lacked spiritual depth and wisdom. We've fully occupied ourselves with debates, arguments, and analysis, but not prayer. If we're doing all this and we're not praying for witnessing power, it's negated. At least some of the time spent in debates, arguments, and analysis could have been spent in prayer. Start praying!

If the Christian church were praying as we should, these troubling current issues would not have such an influence and would not be causing such a distraction. The diagnosis is real; we're prayerless and lacking spiritual answers for how this thing is going to end. Again, God declares, "The nation did not pray to me even though I was always ready to answer…" What we're witnessing today is the result of our prior prayerlessness and now has too many Christians distracted even further from praying. We must start praying!

My Prayer

Father, we know that You're here, ready to answer. Help us to pray. Amen.

What Are Your Thoughts?

What is Your Prayer?

START PRAYING!

DISCUSSION QUESTIONS

1 Can we really depend on prayer to address our societal issues and concerns?

2 How is spiritual power diminished in our society when Christians don't pray?

3 How is it possible for Christians to be involved in current societal debates and still maintain a vibrant prayer life?

WEEK 35
WHEN, IF, AND THEN

"When I shut up the heavens so that there is no rain, or command locusts to devour the land or send a plague among my people, if my people, who are called by my name, will humble themselves and pray and seek my face and turn from their wicked ways, then will I hear from heaven and will forgive their sin and will heal their land."

—2 CHRONICLES 7:13-14 (NIV)

For those Christians who engage in serious praying, our focus text is one of the most used to set the tone for prayer or to call God's people to pray. It is one of my favorites also because it has such remarkable promises. What I like about God is that His promises are always conditional—I know exactly what I must do and what He will do in return. His is a clear and unambiguous contract.

In other words, God is like a good parent to us His children. As earthly parents, we're too quick to make promises without holding our children responsible; we require nothing from them in response to our assurances. Such parenting sets up our children for failure. Not so with God, He will always hold us to a higher standard of living by challenging us to be faithful to Him before He honors His promise.

Like a vigilant parent, God knows His children and their propensity to sin—to turn away from Him. When we do sin, God will do whatever is necessary to save us. At times He will remove His blessings and permit Satan to bring suffering upon us. He said, ***"When I...."*** This is God's way of getting our attention and prompting us to pray so that He can activate His promises. He wants to bless us but cannot favor us while we continue in sin. As a result, He will send spiritual, physical, emotional, and social droughts, locusts, and diseases into our lives. Look around and you'll notice that God is trying to get our attention. The things we're experiencing today are all happening for a reason.

God wants our attention. When He does get it, He desires a response before He honors His promise—***"If...."*** Notice that the response must come from Christians—"my people, who are called by my name." Too often we look to everyone else to solve the problems in our society while Christians remain silent and inactive in our churches. When we do speak up or become active, we miss the mark. Herein is the Christian's voice and action: we must humble ourselves, pray, seek God's face, and repent of our sins. The key in this "if" is praying Christians. Prayer is simply communication with God. The communication is meaningless, however, except we approach God humbly, are eager to have a face-to-face conversation, and abandon any actions or thoughts that might lead to further sinning.

The offer is squarely on the table: ***"then..."*** *Then* is an adverb, which means "as a consequence of, soon afterwards, at that precise time, immediately." Like that wise parent trying to reinforce positive behavior, God's retort to our response is precise and immediate. Look closely, there is no time constraint placed on this promise. Humble, face-seeking, repentant prayer will be heard, and in God's grace and mercy, we will be forgiven and experience healing from the spiritual, physical, emotional, and social droughts, locusts, and diseases. When? Immediately. God simply said, "then will I hear from heaven and will forgive their sin and will heal their land."

My Prayer

Father, we thank You for Your wooing and promise to hear, forgive, and heal. Amen.

What Are Your Thoughts?

What is Your Prayer?

Discussion Questions

1 Why does God allow difficulties in our lives and then tell us to pray?

2 What is likely to happen if Christians pray when the world is facing difficulties?

3 Should we always expect healing in the land when we pray?

MONTH 9

Week 36

Fully Armed, but Prayerless

"Do all this in prayer, asking for God's help. Pray on every occasion, as the Spirit leads. For this reason keep alert and never give up; pray always for all God's people."

—Ephesians 6:18 (GNT)

The phrase "armed and dangerous" has been the theme for numerous songs, a movie, and video games. Most of us are familiar with the expression as it relates to law enforcement. When a criminal is on the run with a weapon, usually armed with a gun, law enforcement will describe him or her as being "armed and dangerous." They're saying to their colleagues and to the public: "Be careful, protect yourself! This criminal has a weapon and will use it." In other words, they've pulled the trigger before, and they're likely to pull it again.

Do you know any spiritually dangerous Christians? Some of us have never pulled the trigger of prayer, and we're unlikely to pull it even now. Consequently, when the Devil encounters most Christians, he's not afraid of us. Yes, I said it. We pose no real threat to him. Why? Because we're fully armed but prayerless. Prayer is a weapon that most of us do not use. Accordingly, we pose no significant threat to the Devil. If someone was attacking you and you had a weapon, you would use it. Well, the Devil is attacking us, and prayer is a weapon, that we're not using.

Dennis Smith reminds us, "Every Christian is involved in warfare against the enemy with eternal consequences at stake."[1] Yet we've become incapacitated by our superficial success (preaching, large churches, television shows, music programs) and have holstered our weapon of prayer. We're at war. That's the bad news. Here's the good news: we can be fully equipped for the war. God has provided all that we'll need to be victorious in the war. Here's my concern, however; it's one thing to be equipped—armed—it's quite another thing to use the weapon. Are you a real warrior?

In Ephesians 6, Paul lets us know that the elements of the war are beyond human comprehension—it's a fight against spiritual wickedness. As such, he outlines our defensive and offensive moves. This is how you conduct yourself in this spiritual war. This is your secret to victory. He begins by telling us (vv. 11, 13) to "put on the whole armor of God…" Just in case we didn't get it, Paul reminds us of the nature of the war we're in. "For we wrestle not against flesh and blood, but against principalities, against powers, against the rulers of the darkness of this world, against spiritual wickedness in high places" (v. 12).

The war is real. If it were not, armor would not be necessary. Moreover, it's not just any type of armor. This spiritual warfare requires spiritual armor. You can't fight a spiritual war with temporal armor. The following lists the six pieces of armor of God that will allow us to stand in the evil day. Paul outlines these pieces of armor in verses 14-17…

- Verse 14: "Stand therefore, having your loins girt about with truth…" Without the belt—the truth of God—our spiritual movements are hampered, and we have no restraint.
- Verse 14: "…and having on the breastplate of righteousness." Too many Christians' hearts are exposed in this spiritual war because we're fighting without the covering of the breastplate—the righteousness of Christ.
- Verse 15: "And your feet shod with the preparation of the gospel of peace…" Christians in this spiritual war cannot afford to be found barefooted on the battlefield. We must be prepared, resolved as to the gospel of Christ.
- Verse 16: "Above all, taking the shield of faith, wherewith ye shall be able to quench all the fiery darts of the wicked." Christians should not enter into this spiritual war without the shield of faith. Our faith must be active in this spiritual war.
- Verse 17: "And take the helmet of salvation…" As we enter spiritual warfare as Christians, we must secure our heads (minds) with the helmet of salvation: we have this hope—salvation in Jesus Christ.
- Verse 17: "…and the sword of the Spirit, which is the word of God." Too many Christians are trying to engage the Enemy with hopes of winning this spiritual war without studying God's Word. It will never happen.

I want you to notice five amazing things about the armor:

First, keep in mind that each piece of armor had a specific purpose, and that there is some logical sequence as to the presentation of the armor. A soldier would first put on his belt, then breastplate, boots, shield, helmet, and sword. ***Second***, we must put on each piece of armor as we prepare to engage in spiritual warfare. These items are useless if not worn.

Third, notice that there is no armor for our back. When we enter into spiritual warfare, we cannot turn our backs on the enemy; we can't turn and run. If we do, we leave ourselves exposed. We have to arm ourselves, stand, face the Enemy, and fight in God's power and might until the end. **Fourth**, observe that the first five items (the belt, breastplate, boots, shield, and helmet) are all defensive armor. We're not going to attack and defeat the Devil with a belt, breastplate, boots, shield, or helmet. **Fifth**, while the sixth item (the sword) is also defensive, it's the only offensive piece of armor. In spiritual warfare, God's Word is our only offensive weapon. We cannot engage the Devil offensively without the Word.

Are you a real a warrior? Because real warriors pray. Unfortunately, putting on the full armor is where most of us stop and wrongfully so. As good Christians engaged in spiritual warfare, we're standing and we're fully armed, but it does not end there. There is another verse. As if all the above directives were not enough to ensure victory, Paul provides this final instruction. Here is the final command that will allow us to stand against the Devil. Look at verse 18, our focus text. Paul says, "Do all this in prayer, asking for God's help. Pray on every occasion, as the Spirit leads. For this reason, keep alert and never give up; pray always for all God's people."

In sum, Paul is saying to us stand courageously, fully armed, but this one additional thing is necessary for victory in spiritual warfare: prayer. Some of us are armed, and we think we're dangerous; we have a false sense of security in this spiritual war. If we're armed (belt, breastplate, boots, shield, helmet, and sword) and we're not praying, our defensive systems are weak, and our offensive systems are inefficient. Being fully armed does not guarantee success in spiritual warfare. We can be fully armed and still lose spiritually and physically because we're not praying.

Many of us are able to quote verbatim verses 10-17 of Ephesians chapter 6, but we've never taken the time to read, memorize, or apply verse 18 while at war. The first thing it says is "do all this"—all what? Put on the belt, breastplate, boots, shield, helmet, and sword—"in prayer." Too many Christians are trusting in the armor and not in the Provider of the armor. Don't put on the armor and become overly confident in the armor and forget that we must remain reliant upon God—*"Do all this in prayer, asking for God's help."*

Further, we're instructed to *"Pray on every occasion...."* As Christians engaged in spiritual warfare, we often pick and choose if and when we want to pray or need to pray. Our praying, however, must be as the *"...spirit leads."* Again, don't become too confident in the armor and neglect to follow God's leading. Any soldier can dress for war and go onto the battlefield fully protected. He is more likely to defect, however, if he cannot trust the leading of his commander. The commander (God) knows the strategy for victory; thus the soldier is expected to follow His lead despite being fully armed.

Finally, Paul instructs us to *"...pray always for all God's people."* Pray always... Whatever else may change, prayer must, and in particular, intercessory prayer must continue and be a constant. Intercessory prayer is an important aspect of spiritual warfare. We're admonished to confirm that all our brothers and sisters are fully armed and that we're praying for them. Jeff Calhoun notes that "when we shirk our duty in God's army to pray and seek Him daily, what invariably happens is that we drop our guard and get suddenly and unexpectedly blind-sided by a spiritual ambush."[2]

Hence, all the pieces of our Christian armor must be buckled on by prayer. "Soldiers of Christ, arise, and put your armor on... From strength to strength go on; wrestle, and fight, and pray..."[3] Belt, the truth of God. The breastplate of righteousness. Shoes, the preparation of the gospel of peace. The shield of faith. The helmet of salvation. The sword of the Spirit—the Word of God. Buckle them on with prayer. We're at war; this is spiritual warfare. This is for keeps. This is a fight to the end. Don't get caught fully armed, but prayerless.

My Prayer

As we fight our spiritual battles, Father, help us to be fully armed and prayerful. Amen.

What Are Your Thoughts?

What is Your Prayer?

DISCUSSION QUESTIONS

1 Are some Christians putting too much trust in the armor and far too little in prayer?

2 Why is it important for real warriors to pray despite being fully armed?

3 What are some ways that Christians are fully armed, but still prayerless?

Notes

[1] Dennis Smith, *Spirit Baptism and Prayer* (spiritbaptism.com), 2008, 28.

[2] Jeff Calhoun, *Armed and Dangerous* (The Christian Broadcasting Network: *https://www1.cbn.com/devotions/armed-and-dangerous*).

[3] Charles Wesley, *Soldiers of Christ, Arise* (Public Domain), 1749.

Week 37
The Progression of Sin

Blessed is the man that walketh not in the counsel of the ungodly, nor standeth in the way of sinners, nor sitteth in the seat of the scornful. But his delight is in the law of the LORD; and in his law doth he meditate day and night.

—Psalm 1:1-2 (KJV)

O ur focus text clearly demonstrates that there is a vast difference between the righteous man and the unrighteous man. As Christians and in our human desire to treasure the good in all things and most individuals, we often have a difficult time with the concepts of "righteous" and "unrighteous." While seeing the good in all is commendable, similarly we're obligated to face reality and accept the truth. There is holiness, and there is also sinfulness. Know, however, that neither surfaces overnight; there is a progression. Psalm 1:1 outlines the progression of sin—separation from God.

First, we find ourselves walking with the ungodly. As we conform to the ways of the world, we become careless about spiritual matters, and we disregard God. Our religious and spiritual slackness causes us to lose our fear of God, but we remain nonchalant. No problem, we're just walking with individuals who are spiritually slack—the ungodly. At first, the separation is so nonthreatening to us and others that we skillful ignore it; we find ways to politely excuse it.

Second, we're no longer walking with the ungodly; we're now standing with sinners. As time progresses the separation from God continues; we're no longer moving. We've stopped to linger with sinners. At this point, carelessness gives way to sin, and sin is transgression of the law. We're now in open rebellion of God's instructions. Unchecked ungodliness leads to willful disobedience of everything that God holds dear.

Third, we take our seat with the scornful. Sinners are worse than the ungodly, but scorners are the worst of sinners. Scorners are not spiritually careless or slack; they openly mock religion and make fun of sin. There is a total disregard for truth—the person despises God. Adam Clarke notes that the scorner's conscience is seared; he/she is now a believer in all unbelief.[1] The progression of sin reaches its zenith, and separation from God is now complete.

This progression is real but avoidable. How can we avoid walking in the counsel of the ungodly, standing in the way of sinners, and sitting in the seat of the scornful? Psalm 1:2 is instructive: "delight in the law of the LORD and meditate on it day and night." Those who take pleasure in God's law and desire to keep it holy are able to avoid the progression of sin. Furthermore, he/she meditates on the law. To *meditate* means "to think deeply or focus one's mind for a period of time." To avoid sin and the progression of sin, we must become intimate and preoccupied with God's Word. While meditation, per our definition, occurs for a period of time, we're charged here to think on God's Word day and night. A habitual and continual focus on the Word is necessary for righteous living.

As there is a progression to sin, there is also a progression to holiness. So, here is another question as I close: how does a person come to love God's Word so deeply to the point that he/she is able to avoid the progression of sin? Answer: prayer. The prayerless Christian is careless with God's laws and has no interest in following them. Face it; it's difficult to take pleasure in or to have a desire for the guidelines of someone when you don't have a relationship with the person. Those who pray sincerely, walk godly; those who don't, don't.

If you're not meditating on God's Word, what exactly are you praying? A praying Christian can usually be found feasting on God's Word. Prayer and a love for God's Word are not mutually exclusive. The habitual and regular life of prayer leads to a habitual and regular of study. As I communicate with God through prayer and develop a relationship with Him, I come to know His standards, and I do my best to live within those standards. This method of spiritual engagement (prayer and meditation on the law) with God provides power to resist the progression of sin. That is, walking with the ungodly, standing with sinners, and ultimately sitting with the scornful.

My Prayer

Father, help us to avoid sin and the progression of sin. Amen.

What Are Your Thoughts?

What is Your Prayer?

Discussion Questions

1 How does a person's prayer life lead to a progression of holiness and not sin?

2 What is the relationship between our prayer lives and our spiritual lives?

3 How does meditating on God's Word influence our prayer lives?

Notes

[1] Adam Clarke, *The Adam Clarke Commentary* (*https://www.studylight.org/commentaries/acc/psalms-1.html*), 1832.

Week 38

Delivered?

So Peter was kept in jail, but the people of the church were praying earnestly to God for him.

—Acts 12:5 (GNT)

For some of us Amazon and more specifically Amazon Prime is the best modern service—the greatest thing since sliced bread. We're shopping online, but we're not home to get the stuff. Well, we're not home because we're busy working to pay for all the items we're buying online. Most of these packages are delivered by UPS, FedEx, or the US Post Office. While we're not at home to get these packages, we confidently continue to work, knowing that all will be fine. Why? Answer: Package Tracking. When we track the package and it says "delivered," we fully expect to come home or arrive at the office and find the package.

Nevertheless, somehow, when we pray and God delivers, we doubt. We question, "Really, delivered?" Many of us would love to have confirmation—proof. Unfortunately, there is no prayer tracking software or app available in heaven's App Store. Faith is the only prayer tracking app that I'm aware of, and like I said, you won't find it in any app store. The developer programmed the app within each of us.

In our focus text, Peter is arrested, but not killed; he was kept in prison. Many of us are in bad situations, but we're still alive. We're being kept in prison. It may be a prison allowed by God or a prison of our own making. At times we will be placed in spiritual, physical, emotional, and/or social prisons, and we'll wonder why. *Why is this happening to me?* Know that God is preserving your life. As such, you'll be arrested and placed in prison.

God could have allowed the Devil to kill you, but He kept you in prison. You don't like it, but you have to trust God. You might be feeling as if God has abandoned you. You're asking, "Why me?" Just remember that Peter was kept in prison. While in your prison, you can be confident in these four things: (1) prayer is being made for you (2) without ceasing (3) by the church (4) to God.

When church members are praying without ceasing to God for you, you usually don't expect any shenanigans from the praying members. But we're dealing with humans without a prayer tracking app—church members without much faith. Consequently, when God delivers, we question, and we doubt. When God delivers you from your prison, church members (praying believers—those praying for you without ceasing to God) will unfortunately have three faithless responses.

First, members will lose their composure (v. 14). Some members will be overcome with joy. And that's good. But you can't get so excited to share what God has done that you lose your ability to function properly—too excited, as if you were not expecting it. It's as if we did not expect God to answer and now that He has. Since we don't know what to do, we lose our composure. While we should get excited about what God did and is doing, we should never be surprised when He moves. Because she had been praying, Rhoda upon hearing Peter's voice should have opened the door and welcomed Peter with these words: "We've been waiting for you."

Second, members are going to think you've lost your mind (v. 15). When you tell church members that God has answered your prayers (explicitly their prayers), they'll call you insane. "You must be out of your mind." Instead of believing that God actually heard and answered our prayers, we often conjure up all manner of explanations because of our lack of faith. Some church members will insist that prayers were answered, but others will call them crazy and then begin to make excuses: "It must be his angel. Can't be him, you've lost your mind."

Third, members will be astonished (v. 16). These church members were having a prayer meeting. Peter's current prison situation was their focus. Nevertheless, when he showed up at the door, they were amazed. They were shocked to see him. How can we be caught off guard (surprised) when we're praying, and the answer comes? The answer to this question is simple: we're praying without much faith.

When we pray without faith, we leave the "answer" at the front door knocking... (v. 16). This is why we can't just pray; we have to pray with faith, believing that God will hear and answer our prayers. Charles Spurgeon notes, "Our unbelief is the greatest hindrance in our way; in fact, there is no other real difficulty as to our spiritual progress and prosperity."[1] And then he asked this question: "Is everything possible except believing in God?"[2]

As I have already noted, many of us are being kept in spiritual, physical, emotional, and/or social prisons. In spite of us, God is hearing and answering our prayers, but we're not being good witnesses. We're too busy looking for proof. The world is looking to Christendom for assurance of answered prayers, but we're unable to bear a true witness as to the power of God because we're stunned ourselves that God actually answered our prayers.

The Christian community must prayer. Moreover, we must pray with confidence. A praying Christian (church) should never be surprised by the moving of their Almighty God—the same God that we've prayed to for assistance. It's unfortunate, but many Christians are praying without faith. As you pray, tell the skeptics "Hold your peace" (v. 17) and let the prisoner know that freedom is coming. Somebody somewhere is praying for you. Delivered? Yes!

My Prayer

Father, help us to pray and have faith, knowing that You have delivered for Your people since the beginning of time. Amen.

What Are Your Thoughts?

What is Your Prayer?

Discussion Questions

1 Is it possible for our prayers to actually open prison doors?

2 Why is it important for Christians to pray and have faith?

3 What should Christians do when they have prayed, but God does not deliver?

Notes

[1] Charles Spurgeon, *Faith Checkbook Daily Devotionals* (*http://www.crosswalk.com/devotionals/faithcheckbook/faiths-checkbook-december-9-11561108.html*), December 9.
[2] Ibid.

Week 39

Wait for It

And when they came together, he gave them this order: "Do not leave Jerusalem, but wait for the gift I told you about, the gift my Father promised."

—Acts 1:4 (GNT)

If you have a Facebook account, I'm sure you've watched a video posted by one of your many friends. Some of those videos are two to three minutes long, but the significant, funny, or alarming portion is toward the end. Your friend would like you to keep watching until the end. So, in the caption for the post, the person will note, "Wait for it." In other words, be patient; it's coming, it's worth the wait, you don't want to miss this—wait for it. Many of us usually follow the instructions, and we'll watch the video to the end. Sometimes we're satisfied. Other times we're disappointed. We feel like we've wasted our time—time we'll never be able to get back. I want to let you know that when God instructs you to wait for it, you'll never be disappointed.

Whenever God tells you to wait, something good is coming—expect something great! In our focus text, Jesus ordered His disciples to wait for it. They were to wait in Jerusalem for the Holy Spirit. This directive—wait for it—creates enormous problems for most Christians if they're not talking about, preaching about, or praying for the Holy Spirit. There is only one way to get this gift from God—you have to pray for it. Ellen G. White ask, "Since this is the means by which we are to receive power, why do we not hunger and thirst for the gift of the Spirit? Why do we not talk of it, pray for it, and preach concerning it?"[1]

Reception of the Holy Spirit is tricky for many Christians because we don't like to wait. When or if we decide to wait, we stand around and do nothing. Someone is saying, "But I'm waiting; you told me to wait." Understand, however, that there is a difference between simply waiting and spiritual waiting. The reason many of us do not have the things we need in life, and in particular the Holy Spirit, is because we're not engaged in spiritual waiting. God is saying to us, "Why are you standing around here?" "Why are you waiting here?" Spiritual waiting for the Christian in this context is to: (1) Move from your current situation; you're out of position (2) Return home; you have to go back to your spiritual base, and (3) Start praying.

First, *move from your current situation; you're out of position.* In Acts 1:9 and 10, Jesus is ascending, and the disciples are standing around watching. I can imagine that they're waving goodbye as the distance between the earth and the bottom of His feet grows wider and wider. They're still watching as His head disappears into the cloud. His torso, legs, and finally His feet disappear into the clouds. And the disciples are still standing around watching.

At this point two men dressed in white appeared and asked the disciples a pointed question (v. 11): "What are you doing standing around here?" Theirs was not a rhetorical question. It was a question that demanded an answer from each and every one of the disciples. "Peter, John, James, Andrew, Philip, Thomas, Bartholomew, Matthew, why are you still standing around here?"

In other words, go now and ask (pray) for, go now and seek the promised gift, go now and wait for the Holy Spirit—you've got work to do. Why are you still standing around here?

Remember? Jesus said to them (v. 4), "Do not leave Jerusalem, but wait for the gift I told you about, the gift my Father promised." Where you're standing is *not* Jerusalem. This is the Mount of Olives. You're close to Jerusalem, but this is *not* Jerusalem. "What doest thou here?" This was the same question that God posed to Elijah (see 1 Kings 18 and 19). After his spiritually high experience on Mount Carmel, Elijah is now running and hiding from Jezebel.

Why is it that after some of your most spiritually high moments, you find yourself in places you should not be? Consequently, you are out of place to receive the Holy Spirit. When Jesus gives you instructions, you have to follow His explicit instructions. If you're going to get His gift, you'll have to move from where you are now to where He wants you to be. You're not in the right place physically, emotionally, socially, or spiritually. Where you are today may be your current situation or position, but it's not where God wants you to be. Move from your current situation! God wants to give you the promised gift, but you're not in the right position to ask—to pray for it. You've got to move!

Second, *return home; you have to go back to your spiritual base.* Verse 12 simply says: "Then the apostles went back to Jerusalem from the Mount of Olives, which is about half a mile away from the city." There was no questioning, no complaining, no fussing; they left "home" and returned to their spiritual base. What do you mean? Well, their present location was home (their former residence, i.e., hometown). The angels did call them "men of Galilee." All the remaining disciples were Galileans—men of Galilee. So, their current position was home.

Now that Jesus was gone, the disciples in their human state (like many of us) would have wanted to stay at home—close to family and close to friends. But the instructions from Jesus were clear: Jerusalem—not Galilee. Notice also the distance from Galilee to Jerusalem was only about half a mile—a very short walk. They were right there, close enough to Jerusalem. The disciples could have said, "Man, we'll just hangout here; we're home." They could have said, "I know He said Jerusalem, but we're close enough. If anything happens, we can get to Jerusalem very quickly; it's only half a mile away."

Again, it's your lack of obedience to God's commands that has resulted in many of your current negative situations—yes, your current situation. You don't have the promised Holy Spirit because you're not in the right place—physically and/or spiritually. Andrew Murray notes, "Obedience was essential as a preparation for the reception of the Spirit."[2] If you've not moved and returned to your spiritual base, you're being disobedient. You're out of place! Get this: most times when you're away from your spiritual base, you're not thinking about or praying for the outpouring of the Holy Spirit. Prayer is the last thing on your mind.

I'm encouraged by the obedience of the disciples. Verse 13 says, "They entered the city…" They're back! They're back in Jerusalem. They're back in the city where Jesus was shamed, where He suffered, and where He was crucified. This place, Jerusalem, was their spiritual base, but it was also the place of their greatest danger and their greatest challenge. Sometimes, your spiritual base (the Christian community) is going to be the place of your greatest danger and challenge. I know you don't want to hear that, but it's true.

Nevertheless, Jerusalem was also the place where Jesus ministered and where He rose from the dead. I know there are some bad memories in Jerusalem. I understand your concerns about not wanting to go back. But the promised Holy Spirit is there in Jerusalem. The power is there. What doest thou here? Why are you still standing around here in Galilee? Move from your current situation and return home to your spiritual base.

Third, start praying. So, they entered the city and went up to the room where they were staying. Verse 14 says, "They gathered frequently to pray as a group…" Here's an important question for you: what do you do while you're waiting for the promised gift of the Holy Spirit? The answer? You pray. The disciples are waiting for the Holy Spirit, and they're praying—praying and waiting. The Holy Spirit is yours for the asking; pray for it! So, how does a command to wait lead to prayer? You may have never noticed, but Jesus never provided any specific instructions about how to get the Holy Spirit. He simply said to them: "Wait, in Jerusalem, for the promised gift." Wait for it.

Now you're wondering, *how did the disciples know to pray for the promised Holy Spirit?* Well, you have to go back to John 14:16. Jesus is speaking to His disciples: "Then I will ask the Father to send you the Holy Spirit who will help you and always be with you." After leaving Galilee, the disciples returned to their spiritual base. When they got back, someone must have remembered what Jesus said in John 14:16. I can hear one of the disciples saying, "Wait, if Jesus promised to ask (pray to) the Father for the gift, why don't we try praying for the Holy Spirit?" In other words, you can never do wrong by doing what Jesus did. Ellen G. White notes, "Although Christ had given the promise to His disciples that they should receive the Holy Spirit, this did not remove the necessity of prayer."[3]

Very often you're faced with challenges in this life, and you stand around looking confused with your back against the wall. You're standing at the edge of the cliff with no real alternatives. You're at the end of your rope and tying a knot is not a feasible option. You're standing at your Red Sea, and you're complaining that you have nowhere to turn. But God is saying to you, "What would Jesus do?" When you don't know what else to do, do what Jesus would do—He prayed.

Too many of us are seeking after the gift, but we have no knowledge of or relationship with the Giver. The disciples never focused on the promised gift but sought the Giver through prayer and the gift—the Holy Spirit—came. The disciples are back at their spiritual base, and they are praying with a single purpose in mind. Ellen. G. White continued her statement: "They prayed all the more earnestly; they continued in prayer with one accord."[4]

When Jesus is telling you to wait for something, there needs to be some level of expectancy. Most of us want to experience the benefits of the Holy Spirit's power to do great things, but we're neglectful in doing what is necessary to get the gift. In other words, we want to have a modern-day Pentecostal experience without doing the necessary work—waiting and praying. Are you willing to do Pentecostal work that will allow you to have a Pentecostal experience? Are you willing to move from your current situation, return to your spiritual base, and begin to pray? Pray for it! Wait for it!

My Prayer

Father, help us to wait. But while waiting, help us to pray for the outpouring of Your Holy Spirit. Amen.

What Are Your Thoughts?

What is Your Prayer?

Discussion Questions

1. Being out of position (place) can impact our prayers. How?

2. What is the relationship between our spiritual base and the effectiveness of our prayers?

3. Why is our Pentecostal experience dependent on our desire to pray earnestly?

Notes

[1] Ellen G. White, *The Acts of the Apostles* (Omaha: Pacific Press Publishing Association, 1911), 50.
[2] Andrew Murray, *Andrew Murray on Prayer* (New Kensington, Penn.: Whitaker House, 1998), 191.
[3] Ellen G. White, *Gospel Workers 1892* (Battle Creek, Mich.: Review and Herald Publishing Co., 1892), 370.
[4] Ibid.

Month 10

Week 40

I'm Only Human

Elijah was the same kind of person as we are. He prayed earnestly that there would be no rain, and no rain fell on the land for three and a half years. Once again he prayed, and the sky poured out its rain and the earth produced its crops.

—James 5:17-18 (GNT)

If you Google the phrase "I'm only human," you'll find several references to songs. The theme of each song, without fail, is about the individual's lack of perfection (failure to achieve or meet some standard) and their ultimate response—"But, I'm only human." Some of us use the same excuse when it comes to prayer, believing that we can't pray and get answers like Bible characters, our grandparents, parents, church members, or friends. We somehow view these individuals as super-spiritual, super-humans and then we use the excuse, "I'm only human" to mask our failure to commit and truly deal with life's challenges through prayer.

Essentially, "I'm only human" is an excuse that James takes away from us at the outset. As we review our focus text, I want to make five points that will challenge and encourage you to abandon this excuse as it relates to Christians initiating and sustaining a meaningful prayer relationship with God.

First, notice that a human offered the prayer for "no rain." Elijah was human. James says he "was the same kind of person as we are." In other words, Elijah was like you and me; there were no differences. He had the same physical, social, emotional, and spiritual limitations and shortcomings. Nothing was supernatural, super-human, or super-spiritual about him. Elijah had no extra advantage. I know you're only human, but this cannot be your excuse. You too can pray like Elijah.

Second, Elijah's prayer was earnest and specific. He was intense and fervent in praying a specific prayer. He prayed, "that there would be no rain." I know you're dealing with concerns, difficulties, cares, trials, and sins in your life. Nevertheless, here are the important questions:

- Have you fixed your focus on those things to pray?
- Are you praying fervently for God to move?
- What are you dealing with right now that you're willing to pray for earnestly and specifically?

I know you're only human, but this can't be your excuse. Be earnest and specific in your prayers like Elijah.

Third, know that your prayers can influence God. Elijah's prayer affected the very course of nature. Through his prayer he disrupted an organic process for three and a half years. God can and will do whatever we've asked Him to do, if we're earnestly praying specifically within His will. It's not foolish to think that God would insert Himself into the difficulties you're dealing with—whether physical, social, emotional, and/or spiritual, if you would only pray. I know you're only human, but this can't be your excuse. Pray like Elijah until you influence God.

Fourth, I want you to trust God. The lack of rain for three and a half years should remind you to trust God. While Elijah prayed a specific prayer for no rain, he never specified a time frame. We must trust God to move how He wants to move when He wants to move. He will always do what is best for us. Even within your earnest and specific prayer, you must allow room for God to be sovereign; allow God to be God. Don't be disappointed when He does something a little different. Trust the process. I know you're only human, but this can't be your excuse. Pray and trust God.

Finally, know that the harvest is coming. Verse 18 says, "Once again he prayed, and the sky poured out its rain and the earth produced its crops." When you pray, God will rain blessings into your life, and it'll yield crops. Through your prayers, He'll produce something of value—fruit, growth, harvest. I know you're only human, but this can't be your excuse. When you pray, God will free you from your drought/famine (concerns, difficulties, cares, trials, sins), and He'll produce something of significant value in your life and in the lives of those around you. I know you're only human, but this can't be your excuse. Pray and wait for the harvest.

Everywhere you turn, someone is telling you that your increase is coming or to name it and claim it, and I agree with them. These individuals are 100 percent correct. What they fail to mention, however, is that there is a process to get your harvest. Here is the process: (1) Develop a relationship with God through prayer (2) Have faith that He will hear and answer your prayers (3) Be patient until He rains blessings into your life, and (4) Then reap your harvest with joy.

"But, I'm divorced." "I'm still living at home." "I'm a single parent." "I'm in debt." "I don't attend church; I'm a sinner." "I'm only human." I understand you're only human, but God is calling humans (you and me) like Elijah to pray. When we (humans) pray earnestly and specifically while trusting in God, we will influence God to rain His blessings into our lives producing a harvest. I know you're only human, but imperfection can't continue to be your excuse for why you're still struggling with the challenges of this life while God is fully able to answer your prayers.

My Prayer

Father, we approach You as humans, trusting that You will provide a bountiful harvest. Amen.

What Are Your Thoughts?

What is Your Prayer?

Discussion Questions

1. Why is it important for us to understand that we don't have to be super-spiritual to pray?

2. Will God always answer our prayer because it's earnest and specific?

3. What does it mean to pray until we've influenced God?

Week 41
Where Is the Answer?

I will answer them before they even call to me.
While they are still talking about their needs,
I will go ahead and answer their prayers!

—Isaiah 65:24 (NLT)

A few years ago at our prayer meeting service, one of our members said something that caught my attention. While I'm sure I've heard it before, I cannot recall hearing the statement in such a realistic way. While what she said was practical, it also left a tremendous spiritual impact in that moment. During our sharing of testimonies, she recounted her prayer for God to intervene in a specific situation. Upon the conclusion of her prayer, she noted that she got up and went looking for the answer. Wow! What faith! What trust!

As I reflected on her testimony, the Holy Spirit reminded me of our focus text: "before they even call to me and while they are still talking… I will go ahead and answer their prayers." What a promise! Like this dear sister, our faith and trust in God should allow us to rise from our knees and commence our search for the answer. We have God's Word that He will provide an answer. After we pray, we should start looking for the answer. As believing Christians, we have every reason to end our prayer and begin the search—where is the answer?

How can we say we have faith, read this passage of Scripture, pray, and have no plan or room for the answer? Here's the reason: many of us are not praying, so this promise means absolutely nothing to us. Those who are praying cannot get excited about the pending answer because of their sins. We know we're not praying within His will. Like the Israelites of old, God cannot hear our prayers because of our sins. The boundless excitement and anticipation of answered prayer is only reserved for those who are praying according to God's will. If you're living and praying within His will, start looking for the answer.

Searching in expectation of an answer is not an indication that God has hidden the answer from us or that we're engaged in a hide-and-seek game with God. A child who makes a gift request and then begins a frantic search leading up to their birthday or Christmas does so because he/she has faith in their parents. Moreover, year after year their parents have never disappointed them. Ending your prayer, rising to your feet, and asking yourself, "Where is the answer?" is a demonstration of your faith and trust in God. Again, if you're living and praying within God's will, commence the search.

God has promised that He will respond: "I will go ahead and answer their prayer." With that guarantee, we should promptly begin to rearrange and restructure our lives to accommodate His response. Too often we pray without expecting a reply, so we don't look for the answer. Many of us are praying for a new car, but we're standing on the used car lot kicking tires. God has already responded; go ahead and look for your blessing.

If you've prayed for water, get a cup.

If bread, get some butter.

If a job, pick out your interview suit.

If a child, start researching names.
If a vacation, request the time off.
If a new car, select a color.

My Prayer

Father, with delight and eagerness we pray and seek Your response. Amen.

What Are Your Thoughts?

What is Your Prayer?

Discussion Questions

1. Is it presumptuous to live as though our prayers are already answered?

2. What does it mean to speak and act in harmony with our prayers?

3. Does praying God's promises put us in a better position to seek answers?

Week 42

Just Say the Word

The centurion replied, "Lord, I do not deserve to have you come under my roof. But just say the word, and my servant will be healed."

—Matthew 8:8 (NIV)

Many of us are hurting. We're ill and suffering in one way or another—physically, emotionally, socially, and/or spiritually. The illness is painful and acute. Our afflictions torment us day and night, and like the centurion's servant, we're ready to die—physically and/or spiritually. Like the centurion in our focus text, we pursue God and pray for healing. While we're praying during our period of sickness, we also need or desire a personal touch. As such, we make plans to see a nurse, doctor, family member, or our pastor must come to us.

The personal touch or medicine cannot and should not be dismissed even as we pray. After the centurion petitioned Jesus, He was assured by Jesus that He would come to his house and heal his servant (v. 7). The centurion prayed but was also assured a personal touch. Likewise, we're counseled that prayer and modern science should complement each other in dealing with any illness. Here is the struggle, however, our lack of faith (not the absence of the personal touch or medicine) sometimes prevents or delays our healing. We know that God has heard our prayer, but He still has to show up under our roof in the form of a nurse, a doctor, a family member, or a pastor. We're expecting a miracle, but it has to be practical.

Guess what? Miracles are not always rational. As a Christian and a believer in the power of prayer, you know that signs and wonders can and will occur at times. Nevertheless, God's Word must be sufficient for you. Can God just say the word? You're looking for a supernatural, light-flashing phenomenon or you get so caught up in the activities (visits, personal touch, treatments) associated with potential healing that you fail to train your ears to hear what God has to say. Do you trust God to just say the word?

Even Martha was lacking this faith. She somehow thought that Jesus would not be able to heal her brother Lazarus without coming to his bedside. "Lord," Martha said to Jesus, "if you had been here, my brother would not have died" (John 11:21). Like the centurion, she could have said to the messengers, "Tell Jesus to just say the word," but she did not. She needed Jesus to come to the house. Don't be discouraged, you're not alone. It takes a special kind of faith to pray for healing and then to humble yourself and say: "Just say the word, and my servant will be healed."

Jesus said to the centurion, "What you believed could happen has happened" (v. 13 MSG). Wow, it's done! "Just-say-the-word" faith is the kind of faith that will make us physically, emotionally, socially, and spiritually whole. "Just-say-the-word" faith is the kind of faith that reaches way back to the beginning. "Just-say-the-word" faith is the kind of faith that expects God to make something out of nothing.

Was it not this same God who spoke the world into existence? He spoke light, water, plants, moon, and birds into existence, and He can speak healing into your life. Yes, there's prayer; yes, there's science; yes, there's personal touch; but I'm trusting in God's Word! Just say the word. When we pray, we would do well to have the centurion's level of faith. Prayer combined with unwavering faith will move God to accomplish much in our lives.

My Prayer

Father, we need a word from You. Just say the word and make us whole. Amen.

What Are Your Thoughts?

What is Your Prayer?

Discussion Questions

1. How should we conduct ourselves after we've prayed for healing?

2. Why is it difficult for us to pray and trust God to just say the word?

3. What is the relationship between prayer, faith, and answers?

Week 43

Only by Prayer

"Only prayer can drive this kind out,"
answered Jesus; "nothing else can."

—Mark 9:29 (GNT)

In our prevailing technologically advanced society, there are a variety of ways to do almost everything. We can hail a taxi by standing on the corner, calling ahead, or by app—Uber and Lyft. Similarly, taking a portrait can be accomplished in numerous ways. For instance, I can go to a studio, I can ask a friend to use his digital camera, and when all else fails, I have my selfie stick. Not only are there a variety of ways to get things done today, the methods are correspondingly progressive. Times have changed, and the number of methods has similarly increased.

Additionally, in the technology, business, and science fields, most experts will tell you that complex problems require complex remedies. We did not get here overnight, and we won't get out of it overnight. The interpretation is straightforward: life is complex, and the solutions must be equally complex. You may not want to admit it, but I'm asking you to be honest with yourself.

You've been dealing with some byzantine challenges over the last several years. Because of the weightiness of your concerns, you've sought multifaceted remedies, attacking the issues from a variety of evolving perspectives. But nothing has changed.

In the background of our focus text, Christ is annoyed with us and lets us know (v. 19) that we should be able to obtain relief from our problems. We cannot, however, because we're not praying. And so He commands us to bring our problems to Him. "Bring him to me." Pray! Many of us are delusional about prayer. We believe that prayer is magical and that when we begin to pray, all manner of challenges will automatically cease. When we begin to bring our problems to God in prayer, Satan will increase his attacks (vv. 20, 26). Prayer is not magical; it is divine. Satan will attack anything that is divine or that is associated with the divine.

This was no simple problem. The complexity of the father's problem is clearly illustrated in verses 17, 18 and 22. As such, we can only assume that this was not the father's first attempt to obtain relief. The gravity of the matter must have forced him to seek out multiple progressive remedies. Jesus, however, asked a very simple question (vv. 19, 21): How long? The question was not asked to assist in diagnosing the problem. The length of time would not be used to determine the appropriate solution. It was a rhetorical question aimed at demonstrating their prayerlessness. Sometimes we're too quick to respond to rhetorical questions instead of thinking about the question.

I like the way The Living Bible puts it: Jesus replied, "Cases like this require prayer" (v. 29). Your prayerlessness, father, since your son's childhood; and your prayerlessness, disciples, since he was brought to you is why he is not healed. These life-changing difficulties can only be resolved through prayer. The father was not a believer; the disciples were believers, "but they couldn't do it" (v. 18). The rules of engagement, however, to remedy life's challenges are the same for both. Whether non-believer and prayerless, partial believer and prayerless, or believer and prayerless, the results are the same: powerlessness!

The father was puzzled. Why can't they heal my son? The disciples were stunned. *Why couldn't we cast out that demon? We have cast out demons before.* The solution was very simple—only by prayer. The father was not praying, and the disciples had stopped praying. The simplicity of the solution can sometimes be perplexing. It can't be that simple! But it is—pray. As Christians, like the rest of the world, we often look for wide-ranging, evolutionary, innovative solutions because we have complicated problems. Yet, genuine believing prayer is the only way to resolve every difficulty. The solution has been and will always be *only by prayer*.

My Prayer

Our trust, Father, is in You. Help us to pray when provoked by the trials of this life. Amen.

What Are Your Thoughts?

What is Your Prayer?

Discussion Questions

1. If we can currently deal with life's challenges in multiple ways, why should we pray?

2. Why is it that Satan increases his attacks when we pray?

3. How is it that we can be disciples (a Christian) and be prayerless?

Week 44

God Still Delivers

When Daniel learned that the order had been signed, he went home. In an upstairs room of his house there were windows that faced toward Jerusalem. There, just as he had always done, he knelt down at the open windows and prayed to God three times a day.

—Daniel 6:10 (GNT)

If you've lived in the United States long enough, you've had issues with the United States Postal Service. At some point you have sent a piece of mail, and it took too long to arrive, or it never arrived. Or maybe mail was sent to you and, again, it took too long to arrive, or it never arrived. Nevertheless, in spite of our concerns and the repeated failure of the mail system, many of us still check our mailboxes every day. Why? Because we expect the service to deliver.

Somehow, when it comes to spiritual matters, we doubt. Somehow, when it comes to trusting that God will deliver for us, we begin to worry. And so, we question, "Can He deliver?" "Will He deliver again?"

Our focus text tells us that the order had been signed. The question remains: "What do you do when the order has been signed." What do you do when the divorce papers, the eviction notice, the termination notice, or the rejection letter has been signed? You've done nothing wrong. And what is happening is happening because you're doing the right thing; you're serving God. What do you do when there's nothing else you can do, but you know God can do everything? You stand!

Like Daniel, there are Christians who've known God to deliver. These Christians who know that God still delivers should behave differently. Allow me to share with you five things that Christians must do, knowing that we serve a God who still delivers.

First, go home; get back to your spiritual base. We read in Daniel 6:10, "When Daniel learned that the order had been signed, he went home." You'll never be able to deal with signed orders if you're not at home—at your spiritual base. A soldier in trouble is told, "Do whatever is necessary to get back to base." Daniel did not go to the king to complain; he went into his house to tell his God about it. Don't go to battle with the Enemy where he has the advantage; get back to your spiritual base. Get back to basics—prayer and Bible study. Get back to what sustained you the last time.

Second, go to your upper room. Daniel 6:10 reads, "In an upstairs room of his house there were windows that faced toward Jerusalem." When the order has been signed, you'll need power. Jesus said to His disciples, "But ye shall receive power, after that the Holy Ghost is come upon you…" – Acts 1:8 (KJV). The disciples were at odds with each other, but they made a conscious decision to go to the upper room. Their upper-room experience resulted in an amazing transformation. The only place I know to get that type of power is in the upper room. The upper room is the place where the disciples received their power, and we can too.

Third, do what you always do. We read in Daniel 6:10, "There, just as he had always done…." As a governor, Daniel had witnessed others being cast into the lion's den. Nevertheless, he did not vary his prayer habit on account of the signed order. The situation is new and we, wrongfully, believe that we must do something new, something unique. Doing what we've always done may seem counterproductive. Don't change anything! Why? Because consistent actions create consistent results. Serving God faithfully will sometimes get you in trouble, but do what you always do anyway.

Fourth, do it publicly. Daniel 6:10 reads, "he knelt down at the open windows…." When the order (e.g., the divorce papers) is signed, many of us stay away from the open window. We stay away from church. We tell ourselves and others, "I'm just worshiping at home." When the order is signed, we need to be deliberately public. We must understand that others are watching us. And based on how we respond publicly, they will come to know Christ, or they'll say no to Christ. Don't go missing; go public. Let everyone (even your enemies) see you're still praising God. Go to your open window and publicly praise God.

Fifth, pray. We read in Daniel 6:10, "and prayed to God three times a day." Trouble did not cause Daniel to pray; prayer got him in trouble. I know you're praying, but when the order is signed, make sure someone else is praying for and with you. Not just anyone—someone who has had an experience with God, who is willing to fast and pray all night, who has enough faith to show up at the den early in the morning. I don't want you praying for me all night if you're going to stay in bed until noon.

No one could recuse Daniel, but the One who delivered him. Sometimes your enemies will seal you in—not once but twice (v. 17). Know, however, that God still delivers. Don't worry about being sealed in. Many of us expect God to operate from outside the den, but we serve a God who is able to operate from within the den. So, when the order is signed, don't give up: get back to your spiritual base, go to your upper room, do what you've always done, do it publicly—pray! Why? Because God still delivers.

My Prayer

Father, may we know without a doubt, that if we pray, You will deliver for us. Amen.

What Are Your Thoughts?

What is Your Prayer?

Discussion Questions

1. What is the relationship between prayer, the upper room, and spiritual power?

2. Can continuing to pray when faced with a new challenge be counterproductive?

3. When the order is signed, instead of praying, why do we doubt?

Month 11

Week 45
Neglected Opportunity

Hezekiah turned his face to the wall and prayed to the Lord, "Remember, Lord, how I have walked before you faithfully and with wholehearted devotion and have done what is good in your eyes." And Hezekiah wept bitterly.

—2 Kings 20:2-3 (NIV)

In our focus text, Hezekiah prays a 22-word prayer reminding God of their relationship. The Holy Spirit interprets the prayer and before Isaiah got to the middle court (v. 4), God responded. God wants to respond in like fashion for you, but He can't if you don't pray. How far away is your middle court—a few minutes, days, weeks, months, or years? In other words, when will God answer your prayer for healing? You'll never know until you pray! God already has a response prepared for your prayer. He has already measured the distance to your middle court, but you'll never know until you pray. You'll never experience God's spiritual, physical, emotional, or social healing power until you pray.

At some period in a 12-month cycle, some companies will provide their employees with a bonus. The amount of the bonus is usually tied to the employee and/or company's performance. In other words, the bonus is usually conditional. God also has a bonus program. Hezekiah (see v. 3) never prayed explicitly for (1) healing (2) a sign that God had healed (3) fifteen more years of life (4) victory in a war with Assyria or (5) protection of the city. But that's the kind of God we serve. Before we call, He will answer. And when God answers your prayers, sometimes, just for fun, He will throw in some extras—a bonus (vv. 4-6). I'm also reminded of Solomon who prayed for wisdom and God threw in unmatched wealth and honor as a bonus (1 Kings 3:5-14).

While God's bonus blessings to us are not restrictive—based on our performance—He expects us to witness about His blessings. When we witness about God's response to our prayers, we open the way to bring others to the knowledge and worship of the God who made heaven and earth. Hezekiah, however, neglected his opportunity (vv. 12-15). He missed an opportunity to bear witness to the power and goodness of God. The ambassadors' main purpose was to inquire about the miracle that the surrounding nations had heard about. Their arrival was not so much to bring him well wishes, as it was to gather information about the paranormal phenomenon.

When God performs a miracle in your life, you've got to tell somebody. My faith is increased when I hear about the answers to your prayers. Most of all God's name is glorified when we boast about what He has done for us. When God heals you, what will others see in your home and in your life? Like Hezekiah, sometimes we take God's blessings for granted. God wants to heal us, but He cannot heal some of us because He can't trust us healed. It is sad, but it is true. God is looking/hoping for a witness, and we're too busy. We're consumed with ourselves and our earthly possessions. Hezekiah missed an opportunity to witness for God. I challenge you, however, to be sure and give God the glory.

When your blessings from God become your god, He will take them all away from you (vv. 16-19). Some of us get so "drunk" with the blessings that we're powerless to recognize and/or acknowledge the source of the blessings. We lose sight of God and fail to discern that we're in danger of losing everything. Our prayers for healing do not have to end with rebuke; let it end with rejoicing. Our prayers for healing will end in rejoicing if we purpose in our hearts to be a witness for God and to give Him the honor and glory.

Too often we neglect the opportunity to allow God to heal us and for His name to be glorified because we don't pray. We turn to everyone and everything, instead of turning to the "wall" and praying to God for healing. Similarly, we neglect the opportunity to give God the glory when He does heal because we don't witness. What an awesome thought that God decided to heal you to reveal Himself to someone else. God wants to heal you because He needs a living witness. When God answers our prayers and heals, our thankfulness should inspire us to tell others of His faithfulness and goodness. Don't neglect the opportunity!

My Prayer

Father, may we exploit every opportunity to glorify and exalt Your holy name. Amen.

What Are Your Thoughts?

What is Your Prayer?

DISCUSSION QUESTIONS

1 When God responds to our prayers, why do we take His blessings for granted?

_____

_____

_____

2 What must be our response when we pray, and God heals?

_____

_____

_____

3 Why is it important for a praying Christian to also be a witness?

_____

_____

_____

WEEK 46

TRANSFORMATION THROUGH PRAYER

About eight days after Jesus said this, he took Peter, John and James with him and went up onto a mountain to pray. As he was praying, the appearance of his face changed, and his clothes became as bright as a flash of lightning.

—LUKE 9:28-29 (NIV)

The transfiguration of Christ that Luke describes in this passage occurred for two reasons. First, God was positioning Christ for His ultimate ministry—His mission of salvation. As a result, His appearance changed and became glorious. Second, the transfiguration revealed to the disciples present that Jesus truly was the Son of God. Christ's change prepared Peter, John, and James to be co-laborers with Him in His mission of salvation. The transfiguration, similarly, prepared them for their mission.

A *transfiguration* is "a transformation; a change in form or appearance—a metamorphosis, a changeover, a conversion." In the context of our focus Scripture, it was an exalting, a glorifying, and a spiritual change. Notice that this new spiritual high for ministry occurred while Jesus was in prayer. Please don't miss this point. The spiritual transfiguration needed for the extraordinary ministry ahead of Him occurred while He was praying. Like Christ, our transfiguration for optimal ministry will not come until we find the time to pray.

Many of us are looking for God to do supernatural, extraordinary things in our ministries (in our personal lives). Know, however, that it must begin with prayer. God is ready and willing to position us for greater ministry, and He also desires to prepare those around us (our fellow church members) to assist Him. Nevertheless, our prayerlessness prevents Him from exalting us, glorifying us, and from bringing about the spiritual change.

Finally, note that you must take others with you to prayer. As you pray, God will position you for effective ministry and will reveal the importance of the same to those with you. Some transformative change is about to happen in your ministry (in your life) and some individuals around you are asleep. Never mind that some may fall asleep (see v.32) or may not be interested; keep praying. God's desire is that we, the collective church, be in prayer for the metamorphosis to take place.

My Prayer

Father, help us to be resolute in our prayers for the transformation that will position and prepare us for a redeeming ministry. Amen.

What Are Your Thoughts?

What is Your Prayer?

Discussion Questions

1. Why is it important for us to understand that the transformation will not occur without prayer?

2. How will ministry change in our churches when we begin to pray for the transformation?

3. What should we do when we're praying for the transformation and others are not supportive?

WEEK 47

PRAYER AND MINISTRY

*The earnest prayer of a righteous man has
great power and wonderful results.*

—James 5:16 (TLB)

E. M. Bounds pointed out that prayer and faith are Siamese twins.[1] If that statement is true, and I do agree, ministry is the third sibling. It is important that we understand the relationship, however. Prayer is not dependent on ministry; however, ministry is dependent on prayer. In other words, they are not codependent. With that foundation in mind, I would like to address three words from our focus text and the adjectives that modify them as it relates to the results of effective ministry—telling others that Jesus saves.

- Earnest (prayer)
- Righteous (man)
- Wonderful (results)

First, earnest describes the type of praying we must engage in to have effective ministry. Matthew Henry notes, "Prayer must go along with all our endeavors for the conversion of sinners."[2] Too often the ministry is the focus at the expense of prayer. While I don't condone it, I understand why. We live in a society of individuals with short attention spans who like to be entertained. Accordingly, we need to keep the attention of our members and potential members. Unfortunately, prayer is not stimulating enough to keep their attention. Thus, the ministry is used to attract attention, and then we may consider praying about it later.

If you want to accomplish significant things in ministry, pray and pray earnestly. There is tremendous importance for praying and having an emphasis on prayer at our various church services. Some of us don't do it, and we need to learn how to pray earnestly. Learning to pray earnestly, however, is like learning to swim; there is no classroom instruction. You only get better at it when you do it; you just have to do it! If we would pray for our ministries like we pray for "things," our ministries would have significant impact on our communities.

Second, righteous describes the spiritual state we must be in to have effective results in ministry. Only righteous men and women can carry out the praying that leads to effective ministries. Many of our prayers are ineffective; hence, our ministry efforts are unsuccessful because of our unrighteousness. "What are you talking about? I have not killed, stolen, lied, or cheated." You continue, "I admit I'm not perfect, but I'm doing my best. I haven't done anything grossly sinful." Herein lies the unacknowledged problem: we've robbed God of His rightful place—His glory.

Robbing God of His glory is sin—unrighteousness. How? Well, too often the ministry is about us and not about Christ. When we're praying for our ministries but stealing God's glory, we're sinning. God will not hear that prayer. We lift up self and not Christ. God will never answer any prayer or bless any ministry if our spiritual state is not right. My church, my preaching, my singing, my program, my, my, my… The third commandment is clear: God is a jealous God (Exodus 20:5).

Finally, wonderful describes the nature of the results we will experience in ministry if we pray in the right spirit—earnestly. Ministry is all about salvation. Our prayers should lead to the manifestation of truth, which produces fruit. Look at how James ends this chapter (James 5:19-20): "My dear friends, if you know people who have wandered off from God's truth, don't write them off. Go after them. Get them back and you will have rescued precious lives from destruction and prevented an epidemic of wandering away from God." That's salvation! When we're praying earnestly and living right, our ministries will accomplish much.

My Prayer

In the name of Jesus, we pray for effective ministry that will yield salvation. Amen.

What Are Your Thoughts?

What is Your Prayer?

Discussion Questions

1 Why is earnest praying necessary for effective ministry?

2 What is the impact of praying, yet sinning on effective ministry?

3 What must be the position of the church, knowing that praying leads to wonderful results in ministry?

Notes

[1] E. M. Bounds, *E. M. Bounds on Prayer* (New Kensington, Penn.: Whitaker House, 1997), 211.
[2] Matthew Henry, *Matthew Henry's Commentary on the Whole Bible* (Peabody, Mass.: Hendrickson Publishers, 1991), 1707.

WEEK 48

IT'S HARVEST TIME

"Pray to the owner of the harvest that he will send out workers to gather in his harvest."

—Matthew 9:38 (GNT)

Jesus is coming soon! Many of us have heard this so many times from so many individuals and on many occasions. Like individuals becoming numb to violence or immune to specific medications, some Christians have become desensitized to hearing about the impending return of Jesus. It's not that we've forsaken our faith and are no longer anticipating His return, we're just not as eager and we've become complacent. It's just another sermon, Bible study, or discussion on the second coming; we've heard it before. Consequently, hearing and talking about His imminent return has become commonplace; it's business as usual.

The meaning and significance associated with His return is not what it used to be. Accordingly, we're not as enthusiastic, and we don't tell anyone to expect His return, and we don't witness. When it comes to the anticipated return of Jesus and joyfully telling others about that return, we can no longer have a business-as-usual attitude. To stem this tide of desensitization, it's important that we do things differently. I'm calling us to prayer as we prepare for Christ's second coming.

Matthew, in chapters 4 and 9, respectively describes the first and second evangelistic tours of Jesus. In all that Jesus did on these tours, His main objective was to harvest souls for His kingdom. As Christians who will no longer engage in business as usual, harvesting souls for His kingdom must also be our main objective. Harvesting is the process of gathering a ripe crop from the fields. It's hard work. Moreover, farmers will tell you that there is a specific time of year and a specific process to harvesting. You can't harvest when you want to and how you want to; there is an ideal time and a correct process to harvesting. So, Jesus commands us to pray.

Our focus text is instructive and equally condemning. There are three points to note:

First, while the needs of the community were countless and many souls were waiting to be reached—to be harvested, He instructed His disciples to pray. If you're not sincerely praying about "it," it's not a priority to you. Some of us are not praying sincerely for family members, neighbors, co-workers, etc. Why? We have yet to see the personal need to pray. Their soul salvation is not a priority to us. As a result, those who are un-churched and under-churched in our communities remain in their current state because we're not praying sincerely for them.

Second, our focus text is condemning to us as Christians because we're trying to do everything but pray. Jesus instructs us to pray, but we're trying to do everything else to gather in His harvest instead of praying. Jesus is saying to us, "Stay in your lane—pray." We want to preach, teach, heal, sing, and conduct community outreach (all good things), but if we're not obedient to His instructions, we will not have sufficient workers for the abundant harvest. As co-laborers with Christ, workers for the harvest is our objective, and your task is to pray.

Third, we must know that God is in control; He is "owner" of the harvest. This is His vineyard. Most of us do not believe and/or accept this simple point: this is His church. We think we're in control, and we want to be in charge of "His" harvest. But the instructions are clear: "Pray to the owner of the harvest that he will send out workers to gather in *his* harvest." He is "the Lord of the harvest." He knows what He's doing; just pray. Too many of us believe that it's our harvest. Harvesting, however, is for the honor and glory of God—the Lord of the harvest.

God, in His wisdom, purposely diminished our initial role in the harvesting process by asking us to first pray. He says, "You pray; allow Me to handle the timing and the process of the harvest." When we pray, it removes the harvesting process from the physical realm and places it in the spiritual realm. Our praying helps Christ to accomplish His spiritual objective—harvesting souls for His kingdom. Jesus preached, He taught, He healed, He showed compassion, and He even restored the dead to life. But He knew that prayer would accomplish much more in the harvesting process than all those things combined. The volume of the harvest is determined initially and chiefly by prayer. The volume of those who will accept Christ as Lord and Savior is determined by our prayers.

The completion of harvesting marks the end of the growing season. The social importance of this event makes it the focus of seasonal celebrations—the harvest festival. As Christians, we sing a hymn in anticipation of our harvest celebration. The refrain says, "When we all get to heaven...."[1] But we all don't get to heaven because we're not praying; souls are being lost. Our lack of praying also delays the harvest festival—the celebration. The refrain continues, "What a day of rejoicing that will be!"[2] That day (getting to heaven, the banquet table, the festival) of rejoicing is delayed because we're not praying.

We've sung this hymn many times, yet we've failed to grasp the implication of the words. When we're so desensitized to the coming of Jesus, good fruit is left to rot on the vine. As a result, we all don't get to heaven, and we delay the celebration. It's harvest time—time for business *unusual*. Are you preparing for the second coming? Are you praying? Are you praying to the Owner of the harvest that He will send out workers to gather in His harvest?

My Prayer

Father, help us to realize that we can no longer engage in business as usual because it's harvest time. Amen.

What Are Your Thoughts?

What is Your Prayer?

Discussion Questions

1 Why was prayer so important to the harvesting process?

2 As Christians, why do we seek to do everything else instead of praying as instructed?

3 Does our lack of praying suggest that we know more about the harvesting process than the Owner of the harvest?

Notes

[1] E. E. Hewitt, *When We All Get to Heaven* (Public Domain), 1898.
[2] *Ibid.*

Month 12

Week 49

Send Me

Then I heard the Lord asking, "Whom should I send as a messenger to this people? Who will go for us?" I said, "Here I am. Send me."

—Isaiah 6:8 (NLT)

If we take a closer look at this narrative, we'll see that it was not until after Isaiah was cleansed (v. 7) that the call came: "Whom should I send as a messenger to this people? Who will go for us?" Oswald Chambers notes, "The call is the expression of the nature of the One who calls, and we can only recognize the call if that same nature is in us."[1] In other words, the Lord is holy and those associated with Him must similarly strive for holiness. This holiness (guilt removed and sins forgiven) can never be reached in our own strength. Like Isaiah, we must acknowledge our need and pray for cleansing.

Furthermore, being holy facilitates our response to His call. Being called by God, hearing the call, and responding as we should has everything to do with our relationship to God—having His nature (holiness). Allow me to go one step further and say that it's not just a relationship, but the *right* relationship. As Christians, many of us have a relationship with God, but it's not the right relationship. Think about it... If you're ever in a relationship with God and you're getting your own way, it is not the right relationship. So, if we're having the right relationship with God, we're holy as He is holy. We will recognize Him and hear His voice; we'll respond accordingly—"Send me."

Many of us are praying to be sent as messengers to the people. God cannot send us, however, until we're cleansed—holy. The path to holiness is found in our having that right connection with God. We can only develop that connection through prayer. The prayer, "Send me" cannot be the first time we've prayed. How can we assume to speak to others for God if we've not spoken to Him? We cannot be strangers with God and direct others to be His friend. Isaiah's connection with God allowed him to respond: "Send me." We need to develop that right connection with God that will allow us to recognize Him, hear His voice, and respond, "Send me." I pray that we will.

Allow me to address those of us who have responded, "Send me" and are now waning from that call. We were cleansed, called, and sent, but now we're looking back. I continue to be amazed by the number of Christians who accepted the call, but years later they find themselves heading in the opposite direction. I always find myself wanting to ask, "What happened to the call? You told us you were called." The main reason we look back is because we're wavering in our relationship with God; we've stopped praying.

In our seasons of prayerlessness, the things we've left behind regain their luster. I don't have the time or space to deal with every aspect of Elisha's call, but you can read all the details in 1 Kings 19:19-21. This is mind-blowing! When Elisha was called, he butchered his oxen, made a fire with the plow, and boiled the meat for a farewell dinner with the family. If you didn't get the spiritual significance of what just happened, here it is: he burned and ate the tools of his former trade. In other words, he had no intentions of going or looking back.

As a result of our prayerlessness, we squander our connection with God, and we become useless to Him as a messenger. We will never be able to pray, "Send me" and similarly will never be able to maintain our commitment to that prayer unless we develop and maintain the right connection with God through prayer. "Send me" is a serious prayer that should not be taken lightly. We had a choice, and we accepted His call. Don't look back! Don't go back! Like Elisha, burn the bridges behind you if you're traveling with God through prayer.

My Prayer

Father, help us to burn those bridges that will lead us back and away from our calling. Amen.

What Are Your Thoughts?

What is Your Prayer?

Discussion Questions

1. Why is prayer such an important part of accepting the call?

   _____
   _____
   _____

2. What role does prayer play in maintaining your connection with Christ after accepting the call?

   _____
   _____
   _____

3. Is it possible to be cleansed, called, and sent without having a prayer life?

   _____
   _____
   _____

Notes

[1] Oswald Chambers, *My Utmost For His Highest Daily Devotional* (*https://utmost.org/the-voice-of-the-nature-of-god/*), January 16, 2019.

Week 50
An End of Praying

*Now when Solomon had made an end of praying, …
the glory of the L*ORD *filled the house. And the priests
could not enter into the house of the L*ORD, *because
the glory of the L*ORD *had filled the Lord's house.*

—2 Chronicles 7:1-2 (KJV)

Have you ever arrived at church for worship and couldn't get in? No, really, think about it. When was the last time you got to church, and it was too crowded for you to get into the church? I know, too many questions. But this final crucial question is not rhetorical and demands thoughtful contemplation and a response from each of us. Was the church too crowded because of the presence of the Lord? When was the last time you got to church and felt crowded because the church was filled with God's presence?

Our focus text says, "Now when Solomon had made an end of praying, …the glory of the LORD filled the house." In such a powerful and noteworthy statement, I want to focus on two words that many may have overlooked or might even find inconsequential—"end" and "filled." On the contrary, these two verbs are consequential as it is the action of "ending" that leads to the "filling." In other words, the filling of the church with God's presence does not ensue without the ending of Solomon's praying.

The verb *end* means "the cessation of a course of action, pursuit, or activity—to bring or come to an end." Wrapped up in the notion of *end* is the accompanying concept of a beginning. Accordingly, to *end* something means that at some point you started. Too often we give prayer lip service and never follow through. We talk about it, we plan for it, but we never actually pray. The laws of nature are clear; you can't end what you've never started. Solomon was able to make an end of praying because he started praying.

God's overwhelming glory was an illustration of His approval and acceptance of Solomon's prayer. Unfortunately, God cannot approve what He does not hear and see. When the church prays and God approves, we will know it. When He approves of our prayers, we will know by the manifestation of His awe-inspiring presence. On a personal level, when God fills us, we can be assured that He approves our prayers. God will never occupy any space or place where He is not welcomed. To be found praying is an indication of our desire to be filled. It means that we've made room for God to fill us. God's presence will fill us when we're actively involved in prayer.

When we pray, God's presence will fill the church. Here is the problem, however: we're not praying, and His presence is not filling our churches. We're not praying, and our churches are filled with everything else but the glory of God. While we (like the priests—v. 2) should not be able to get in because of His tremendous glory, God cannot get into our churches because of our devastating self-centeredness. Some of our churches are crowded (you can't get in), but God's presence is absent. The fact that we don't realize He's missing is even worse. The only way the Lord's presence will fill our churches is that we make "an end of praying." That means we've got to start praying. Again, you can't end what you've never started.

My Prayer

Father, I pray that You will fill us and our churches with Your splendid glory. Amen.

WHAT ARE YOUR THOUGHTS?

WHAT IS YOUR PRAYER?

AN END OF PRAYING

DISCUSSION QUESTIONS

1. When we pray, how will we know that God's presence has filled the church?

2. Why is it that some churches are praying, yet God's presence is absent?

3. Some churches are filled every week, but they're not praying. How is this possible?

WEEK 51

PRAYER MUST GIVE WAY TO ACTION

> *Peter sent them all out of the room; then he got down on his knees and prayed. Turning toward the dead woman, he said, "Tabitha, get up." She opened her eyes, and seeing Peter she sat up. He took her by the hand and helped her to her feet.*
>
> —ACTS 9:40-41 (NIV)

Prayer is about salvation. For most of us, that's a strange concept. "You mean prayer is not just about getting what I want and need from God?" While we have needs, and God throughout His Word has promised to supply those needs, our praying must also be motivated and accompanied by a desire for practical evangelism. In other words, if you're praying for someone to be saved, you also have to take action so that the person can meet this Jesus to whom you pray. Prayer must give way to action. After you've prayed, your actions must have a positive influence and impact on those around you. Praying to reach the surrounding community and doing nothing to reach them is not a spiritually prudent method for effective evangelism.

Luke is writing in Acts chapter 9, and he tells how Peter is traveling throughout the territory of the early church. He makes a stop in Lydda, a place known for its poverty. This reminds me of cities across the United States and even throughout the world known for their poverty. From Lydda, Peter is called to make a stop in Joppa, a seaport city. Like most seaport cities, I can only assume that Joppa was somewhat better off than Lydda. What's the warning? We must be ready to witness to those labeled as underprivileged as well as to those regarded as affluent.

As Christians, we must admit that prayer is the channel through which the church receives its power. Many of us have been in the church for many years. We know all the doctrines—all the dos and don'ts. We know and we sing, "Would you be free from your burden of sin? There is power in the blood."[1] Yet we don't pray; we don't call on the name of Jesus. It's one thing to acknowledge that there's power in the name of Jesus; it's another to actually call on the name of Jesus—to pray.

Luke shares that a woman named Tabitha in Joppa was sick and died. Following the customs of the time, her body had been washed and prepared for burial. Some individuals in our churches and in our communities are dead spiritually, and many of us are just following the customs of our day. We've washed our hands of them, and we're ready to bury them. We've stopped praying for them. We don't believe that prayer is the channel through which the church receives its power that can and will restore life.

Same church, same Christians, but some were preparing for her memorial service, while others saw an opportunity for a miracle. Joppa was not that far from Lydda, and when the believers in Joppa heard that Peter was in Lydda, they sent two men to him with the message, "Please hurry and come to us." Some of us have

PRAYER MUST GIVE WAY TO ACTION

friends and family members who are spiritually dead. We need to stop talking with the funeral director, stop writing the obituary, cancel the memorial service, and start praying.

Peter shows up, and the people are crying and carrying on—some of us behave so badly at funerals. We perform as if we have no hope. That's not the behavior of a true Christian. So, Peter clears the room, and then he prays. Jesus had a similar encounter in Mark 5:39, 40. When He showed up, He told the mourners that Jarius' daughter was not dead, and they laughed at Him. So, he cleared the room. Someone is saying, "These individuals in the community and the church are not spiritually dead; we can reach them, and we can save them." And so, you're praying, but all you hear is laughter. Like Peter and like Jesus, you're going to have to clear the room. You're going to have to pray and ask God to clear the room (yea, the very church) of distractions.

Now that we've admitted that prayer is the channel through which the church receives its power, we must take action. As Christians, we must now agree that prayer must give way to action. Prayer must always give way to action. I recently saw this statement on Facebook: "There's no need to pray all night if there are no planned activities in the daytime." In other words, it makes no sense for us to pray for others to be saved and then do nothing to facilitate their salvation. I know some of you are not on Facebook, so let me come a little closer to home. Ellen G. White says, "Speak and act in harmony with our prayers."[2] Peter didn't just pray; he prayed and then he took action.

You're asking, "Well, what did Peter do? What did he do after he prayed?" Let's take a closer look at our focus text...

- ***He turned toward the dead woman.*** After we've prayed, we must turn toward the sick and spiritually dead in our communities and churches. Turn and face them; don't just walk past and over them.

- *He said, "Tabitha, get up."* After we've prayed, we must call those who are sick and spiritually dead by name. Get to know them and say to them, "Arise, get up; Jesus loves you."
- *He took her by the hand.* After we've prayed, we must extend a hand to the sick and spiritually dead. Don't just extend our theology and our doctrines; extend a loving hand. Don't be afraid to touch them.
- *He helped her to her feet.* After we've prayed, we must offer the sick and spiritually dead in our communities and churches practical help. As a church, we must do whatever is necessary to lift them up.

When we do our part, God will do the rest. When we pray and take action, we'll get results. That's the sequential linear combination that yields effective evangelism. I know you're asking, "What results?" Well, those in the community and church will come to believe. Look at verse 42: "The news about this spread all over Joppa, and many people believed in the Lord." Individuals heard that Tabitha was dead but was now alive, and they accepted Christ as Lord and Savior. When we restore the lives of those in our communities and churches, when we call back to life those that are spiritually dead, word is going to spread, and others will come to accept Him as Lord and Savior.

The only way I know to mend the spiritually sick is to pray. The only way I know to revive the spiritually dead is to pray. We must use prayer—not to ask for more stuff. But we must use prayer to ask God to perform miracles in our communities and churches. And when He does, our responsibility is to act and to keep praying, knowing that enlarged earthly territory leads to an enlarged heavenly kingdom. Prayer must give way to action.

My Prayer

Father, may we, Your people, fully and prayerfully embrace the territory You've made available to us. Amen.

What Are Your Thoughts?

What is Your Prayer?

Discussion Questions

1. If prayer is the channel through which the church receives its power, why aren't our churches praying?

2. What will be the impact on ministry if we actually prayed before acting?

3. What does the author mean by, "Prayer and action is the sequential linear combination that yields effective evangelism"?

Notes

[1] Lewis E. Jones, *Power in the Blood* (Public Domain), 1899.
[2] Ellen G. White, *Christ's Object Lessons* (Hagerstown, Md.: Review and Herald Publishing Association, 1900), 145.

Week 52

I've Prayed, Now What?

The LORD came and stood there, calling as at the other times, "Samuel! Samuel!" Then Samuel said, "Speak, for your servant is listening."

—1 Samuel 3:10 (GNT)

God has a mouth. God has a voice. And so, we can conclude that God does speak. In fact, Tozer points out, "It's the nature of God to speak."[1] Still, many of us find ourselves uncertain as to whether we're hearing God's voice after we've prayed. We're doubtful and we find ourselves asking the question: "How do I recognize the voice of God?"

A careful read of Jeremiah 33:1-3 will establish and confirm the fact that God does speak. God will speak to us at any time—whenever, however, wherever we are. Whatever our situation, wherever our prison, know that God can and will speak to us if we're willing to listen. Keep in mind that sometimes our best work can come from our prison situations.

Not only does God speak, He'll speak as often as necessary. Our disobedience and distrust are the main problems, but God will speak to us until He gets our attention. Oswald Chambers encourages us to "get into the habit of saying, 'Speak, Lord,' and life will become a romance."[2] Now, someone is saying, "Speak, Lord!" Nevertheless, someone else is saying, "How do I know that's God speaking?"

Well, whenever God speaks, He will clearly identify Himself. He said to Jeremiah, "The LORD; the one who made the earth, who formed it, and set it in place. Creator—the LORD is my name." "Now that I have your attention, now that you know who I am, let Me speak to you." God's response is the most exciting part of prayer—and the most important."[3]

God wants to have a dialogue with us. Moreover, He wants to have a relationship with us. If you're expecting to receive answers from God, you have to pray. Subsequently, He promises to tell us things—wonderful, marvelous, incomprehensible things about which we know nothing. These "promises are given not to supersede, but to quicken and encourage prayer."[4] And so God cries out, "Speak to me (pray), and I will speak to you."

It's never the Lord who is not speaking; it's us who are not hearing. "Don't blame God for silence when the real problem is deafness."[5] Remember, God has a mouth. God has a voice. And so, we conclude that God does speak. Still, someone is saying, "Lord, is that You?" Recognizing His voice is not about feelings or emotions, a mindset, your posture or position, a formula, or any gimmicks. Let me now use the narrative found in 1 Samuel 3:1-10 to make five points about recognizing God's voice and ultimately what our response must be.

First, God's voice may be infrequent, but He's never silent. 1 Samuel 3:1 says, "In those days the word of the LORD was rare; there were not many visions." Rare, yet we find God speaking here to Samuel. He spoke before to Adam and Moses. He spoke to Jeremiah in the text. He spoke in the New Testament through Jesus, and He still speaks today. But when we're not living right, we can't hear God. God actually withdraws His presence.

Second, God will call (speak) until He gets your attention. 1 Samuel 3:4, 6, 8, 10 notes, The Lord came and stood there, calling as at the other times, "Samuel! Samuel!" Samuel did not respond appropriately the first three times, but God did not give up. He moved in closer and called his name twice—"Samuel! Samuel!" Despite our waywardness and misgivings about God, He wants to have a relationship with us and will get our attention by any means necessary.

Third, if you don't know the Lord, you will never recognize His voice. 1 Samuel 3:7, "Now Samuel did not yet know the LORD: The word of the LORD had not yet been revealed to him." A husband is generally able to recognize the sound of his wife's voice because he knows her; he has a relationship with her. Over the courtship and now many years of marriage, her voice has been revealed to him over and over. Many of us are still unable to distinguish the Lord's voice because we don't know Him; we don't have a meaningful relationship with Him. Many will ask the question: "How do I get to know God?" The answer? Prayer and Bible study!

Fourth, a prior relationship with God is important to recognizing His voice. 1 Samuel 3:8 notes: "Then Eli realized that the Lord was calling the boy." Eli had a prior relationship with God, but because he had allowed spiritual corruption to come between him and God, he was unable to promptly recognize the voice of God. Notice, it was not until the third time that Eli realized God was speaking. Just because we've walked with God in the past does not mean He'll always speak to us. When we allow individuals and things to come between us and God, He may bypass us and speak to others, and it'll take us longer to recognize His voice.

Fifth, you have to respond when God calls (speaks) to you. 1 Samuel 3:10, Then Samuel said, "Speak, for your servant is listening." After we've prayed, God will speak. When we, like Samuel, recognize that it's God speaking to us, we must be obedient to His directives. Whether He's calling us to a lifestyle change, to build or further grow our relationship with Him through prayer, or to demonstrate spiritual growth, our response must be: "Speak, for your servant is listening."

Note that the voice of God is authentic, clear, and still. "He does not come with a voice like thunder; His voice is so gentle that it is easy to ignore it."[6] Consequently, we can't hear; we will not hear if we're not listening. If you're not hearing God's voice after praying, check your spiritual receiver; turn it on, place your antenna in the right position, and move to the correct frequency. "What hinders me from hearing is that I am taking up with other things. It is not that I will not hear God, but I am not devoted in the right place."[7] I've prayed, now what? Listen and obey!

My Prayer

Father, as we pray, help us to be quiet long enough to hear Your voice. Amen.

What Are Your Thoughts?

What is Your Prayer?

Discussion Questions

1. How important is prayer in the process of hearing and recognizing God's voice?

2. What must we do when we're praying but not hearing God's voice?

3. We're so busy that after praying we're not silent long enough to hear God's voice. What can we do?

Notes

1. A. W. Tozer, https://awtozer.com.
2. Oswald Chambers, *My Utmost For His Highest Daily Devotional* (*https://utmost.org/the-dilemma-of-obedience/*), January 30, 2020.
3. Morris Venden, *The Answer Is Prayer* (Nampa, Id.: Pacific Press Publishing Association, 1988), 145.
4. Matthew Henry, *Matthew Henry's Commentary on the Whole Bible*, (Peabody, Mass.: Hendrickson Publishers, 1991), 1295.
5. Royston Philbert, Personal Communication.
6. Oswald Chambers, *My Utmost For His Highest Daily Devotional* (*https://utmost.org/classic/the-habit-of-a-good-conscience-classic/*), May 13, 2019.
7. Oswald Chambers, Oswald Chambers Quotes on Spiritual Leadership (*http://www.bradbridges.net/2015/06/09/25-oswald-chambers-quotes-on-spiritual-leadership/*), June 9, 2015.

BONUS ESSAY

As you begin a new year, continue your focus on prayer.

Same God!

One time, after they had finished their meal in the house of the LORD at Shiloh, Hannah got up. She was deeply distressed, and she cried bitterly as she prayed to the LORD. Meanwhile, Eli the priest was sitting in his place by the door.

—1 Samuel 1:9-10 (GNT)

Same means "identical, not different—exactly similar." Right? A few years ago, a member at my local church gave birth to identical twins. From birth we knew these girls to be identical—the same. As they grew older and began exploring their new surrounds, I was unable to tell them apart. One day, however, someone decided to help me out by letting me know that one of the girls had a mole on her cheek. While this information was extremely useful in helping me to distinguish between the twins, it was also a little disappointing. In my mind, because of the mole, the two girls were no longer identical—the same.

We serve a God, conversely, who is always the same—identical, not different, exactly similar. The God of the Old Testament is the same God of the New Testament, and He is the same God today. My Bible tells me that Jesus Christ is the same yesterday, today, and forever (Hebrews 13:8). Every good gift and every perfect gift is from above, and cometh down from the Father of lights, with whom is no variableness, neither shadow of turning (James 1:17). He is the same; there is no variableness with Him.

Some of you are struggling financially at work and in your relationships. You're praying and dealing with the distressing reality that over and over again doors of opportunity continue to close in your face. With brimming optimism, you pray and announce, "This is it; this is my time. I've finally arrived"—only to realize that the door has been closed once again. On the other hand, some individuals seem to be in God's favor. Every prayer they pray is answered, and God continues to open every door. Guess what? It's the same God.

As Christians, we fail to recognize and internalize the fact that the same God who permits doors to close is the same God who opens doors. Sometimes it's the same door. I'm going to say more about that later. As you celebrate or curse this God, allow me to make seven points using the narrative of Hannah found in 1 Samuel chapter 1 to help you deal with closed doors.

First, you're going to feel like the second wife (a concubine)—not a priority. Elkanah had two wives, Hannah and Peninnah. Peninnah had children, but Hannah did not (1 Samuel 1:2). While Hannah was the first wife, she felt like the second wife—a concubine—because she had no children. You're the first wife, but the second wife keeps hanging around bearing children for your husband. In this Christian journey, at some point, while praying you're going to feel like the second wife. At times, it seems that God is blessing everyone else, but you're the one praying and worshipping Him faithfully. And so, you begin to question whether you're a priority to God.

Second, you're going to feel short-changed—cheated. Each time Elkanah offered his sacrifice, he would give one share of the meat to Peninnah and one share to each of her children. And even though he loved Hannah very much he would give her only one share (1 Samuel 1:4-5). The second wife received multiple portions, while Hannah felt short-changed; she received a lesser portion. As a praying Christian, you know that God loves you very much, but this peculiar allocation of blessings makes you feel cheated. Keep in mind that sometimes when things are falling apart, they may actually be falling into place.

Third, God closed the door. The Lord had kept Hannah from having children (1 Samuel 1:5). "Many of your afflictions have been visited upon you, in the wisdom of God, to bring you closer to the throne of grace."[1] God is allowing "it" because He wants you to pray. He wants an improved relationship with you. As a praying Christian, you must know that God will sometimes deny you a perceived blessing. Still, the God who said, "I will blow on it," is the same God who said, "I will restore the years that the locusts has eaten up." If God closes a door, stop pounding on it! Trust that whatever is behind the door is not meant for you.

Fourth, people will taunt you to your face. Peninnah, her rival, would torment and humiliate Hannah because the Lord had kept her childless (1 Samuel 1:6). Hannah is the first wife who is feeling like the second wife and feeling cheated as God is closing doors. And now she's being taunted by the second wife. Like Hannah, you've been faithfully praying to God, and you know that He loves you. But still His blessings continue to evade you. When God appears not to have come through for you, those closest to you will taunt you to your face.

Fifth, the taunting will go on for years—right in the very church. This went on year after year. Whenever they went to the house of the Lord, Peninnah would upset Hannah so much that she would cry and refuse to eat anything (1 Samuel 1:7). Whenever they went to church, they would all sit together on the same pew—Peninnah and her children right next to Elkanah and Hannah. Year after year, in church, Peninnah would remind Hannah that she was childless. It's still happening today; church members will not allow you to forget. Year after year, while in church, sometimes from the very pulpit, they'll remind you of how God's blessings have eluded you. So, what do you do when God is the One closing the doors; He's the one denying you the opportunities?

Sixth, you're going to have to cry and pray, "Lord, remember me." She was deeply distressed, and she cried bitterly as she prayed to the Lord. Hannah made a solemn promise: "Lord Almighty, look at me, your servant! See my trouble and remember me..." (1 Samuel 1:9-11). Peninnah had talked about her so bad that all she could do was pray and cry. You're going to cry and pray so hard and so sincerely that individuals (the pastor) at church will think you're drunk. Don't allow anyone to distract you; keep crying, keep praying. Tears are prayers too; they travel to God when you cannot speak. One tear can hold an entire prayer. Never be afraid to let them flow. When you can't find the words to deal with your situation, you can cry.

Seventh, God will remember you right away. "And they rose up in the morning early, and worshipped before the Lord, and returned, and came to their house to Ramah: and Elkanah knew Hannah his wife; and the Lord remembered her" (1 Samuel 1:19). Now they're on their way home from church, Elkanah and Hannah are holding hands in the front seat of the car, they get home, and the Lord remembered her. When God begins to open your doors and begins to bless you, you're going to experience some pleasure. Somebody understands what I'm saying. Here's what is amazing: it's not going to take years, months, weeks, or even days; the blessing is going to happen right away. God is right now making the necessary arrangements to answer your prayers.

Bonus Point: now you offer a prayer of praise while you laugh at your enemies. Hannah prayed. "The LORD has filled my heart with joy; how happy I am because of what He has done! I laugh at my enemies; how joyful I am because God has helped me (1 Samuel 2:1). As a faithful praying Christian, remember that your good plans are not necessarily God's plans. God will close some doors because we're not ready or because we're not living right. In doing so, He will put up this sign: "Temporarily closed for spiritual maintenance." Yes, God will shut doors. But when He opens doors, He opens them in such a spectacular way that only He gets the credit.

Hannah wanted a son, but God needed a prophet. The door that He closed for the son was the same door that He opened for His prophet. The same God who permits doors to be closed is the same God who will open doors. Sometimes it's the same door. The God of the second wife is God of the first wife. The God of the lesser portion is the God of the double portion. The God who shuts up is the God who opens up. The God who permits taunting is the God who produces laugher. The God who shuts up for years is the God who opens up the next day. The God who allowed crying is the God who brings rejoicing. The God you thought had forgotten you is the God who remembers you. Same God—if we would only pray.

My Prayer

Father, help us to trust You—even when You close a door. Amen.

What Are Your Thoughts?

What is Your Prayer?

Discussion Questions

1 What do we do when we've prayed and God continues to close doors?

2 Is something wrong with the praying Christian when God seems to have forgotten him/her?

3 If we're praying for a son but God needs a prophet, what must we do to create a win-win situation?

Notes

[1] Ellen G. White, *Testimonies for the Church Vol. 4* (Mountain View, Calif.: Pacific Press Publishing Association, 1881), 143.

HOUSE OF PRAYER INDICATOR ASSESSMENT

Welcome to an assessment that has the potential to grow the spirituality of your church and change your life for the better.

Some church leaders and members have been duped into removing prayer from the center of their churches and have placed it on the periphery or semi-periphery. In these churches, prayer is not valued, and prayerlessness is the norm. What about your church? Is prayer a priority in your church? Is your church a house of prayer?

This assessment is a tool you can use to help assess the status of prayer in your church. By completing the assessment you'll gain insight into whether your church is a house of prayer. Hold on to your seat; it'll confirm or challenge your beliefs about your church's prayer status.

The assessment is divided into two parts. **Part I** has four sections and **Part II** has four sections. The assessment will take approximately 20 minutes to complete. You'll be presented with statements. Indicate the extent to which you agree or disagree with each statement by using the following options: **Strongly Agree**, **Agree**, **Disagree**, or **Strongly Disagree**. You'll also be presented with questions. Answer **Yes** or **No** to each question.

It is important that you respond truthfully and from your perspective and not try to provide answers that you think others would like to hear. The objective is to get a true status of prayer in your church, from your point of view.

The journey to spiritual change begins now! Ready to get started?

PART I

Section One	Strongly Agree	Agree	Disagree	Strongly Disagree
Prayer is the fundamental biblical principle that should guide a church's activities (its ministries and programs).				
The church's prayer life (its commitment to prayer) can positively impact the surrounding community.				
The level of spiritual growth in a church can be strengthened through corporate prayer.				
Prayerless Christians (church members) can impede the proper functioning of a church.				
A prayer strategy should lead the spiritual, membership, and financial growth strategy for a church.				

Section Two	Yes	No
Is there a spiritual environment in your church that supports prayer and prayer related activities?		
Does your church have a prayer champion(s), i.e., someone with a profound understanding of the importance of prayer in God's house (your church) and supports it?		
Does your church view individuals, practices, and/or things that are hindering its spiritual growth and development as a threat?		
Is your church recognized by the community as a place of prayer?		
Is the attendance at prayer meeting worship service significantly lower, when compared with other worship services?		

HOUSE OF PRAYER INDICATOR ASSESSMENT

Section Three	Strongly Disagree	Disagree	Agree	Strongly Agree
Cultivating and maintaining an organizational culture and worship structure where consistent corporate and personal prayer is the norm, is practiced at my church.				
In my church, prayer plays a prominent role in the lives of members and chiefly in the lives of church leaders.				
My church is not simply going through the motions, and focuses on genuine prayer and worship, week after week.				
My church does not need to change its assumptions, ways of thinking about, and approach to prayer.				
My church's primary function, first and foremost, is to be a house of prayer.				

Section Four	Yes	No
Is prayer worship?		
If your church were to schedule a prayer meeting service and a game night, would the attendance at game night be better?		
Is prayer included in the mission and vision statements of your church?		
Are the church's ministries adding spiritual value to the community?		
Does your church spend quality time in prayer at committee and planning meetings?		

PART II				
Section Five	Strongly Disagree	Disagree	Agree	Strongly Agree
I think prayer, as a central worship practice, has been removed from the center of my church.				
The legacy of prayerlessness in my church is negatively impacting our surrounding community.				
I've witnessed that there is a correlation between my church's spiritual weakness and its lack of corporate prayer.				
Prayerless Christians (church members) are impeding the proper functioning of my church.				
A prayer strategy is not leading the spiritual, membership, and financial growth strategy for my church.				

Section Six	Yes	No
Is the level of unity (oneness, one accord) great among members at your church?		
In your church, is more time allocated for Bible study, singing and/or preaching, when compared to time spent praying?		
In your church, are the youth and children excited about prayer?		
Do all of the worship services in your church reflect prayer as a priority?		
Are there individuals, practices, and/or things in your church preventing it from moving forward spiritually?		

HOUSE OF PRAYER INDICATOR ASSESSMENT

Section Seven	Strongly Agree	Agree	Disagree	Strongly Disagree
Churches should cultivate and maintain an organizational culture and worship structure where consistent corporate and personal prayer is the norm.				
Prayer must play a prominent role in the lives of church members and chiefly in the lives of church leaders.				
Churches should avoid the pitfall of simply going through the motions, week after week, when it comes to genuine prayer and worship.				
Churches that are serious about prayer, usually change their assumptions, ways of thinking about, and approach to prayer.				
The church's primary function, first and foremost, is to be a house of prayer.				

Section Eight	Yes	No
During the last 3 months, have you preached or heard your pastor preach a sermon on prayer?		
Does your church have a weekly prayer worship service where prayer, and only prayer, is the focus?		
Are your members and visitors excited about prayer?		
Does your church have and use prayer request cards and/or a prayer box?		
Does your church have a vision for prayer (i. e. a clear awareness of what can and will happen when you and other members pray)?		

You've completed our House of Prayer Indicator Assessment. Thank you for valuing your church and for investing your time in completing the assessment.

Please refer to the scoring grid (pages 340-343) to calculate your assessment summary score. For example, Part I, Section One, first statement: if you responded "Strongly Agree" give yourself 2.5 points, etc. Similarly, Part I, Section Two, first question: if you responded "Yes" give yourself 2.5 points, etc.

Total your score from each section and insert the value on each line below. Finally, add the totals from each section together for your assessment summary score. Summary scores for our House of Prayer Indicator Assessment can range between 20-100.

(1) ___ + (2) ___ + (3) ___ + (4) ___ + (5) ___

+ (6) ___ + (7) ___ + (8) ___ = ___

HOUSE OF PRAYER INDICATOR ASSESSMENT

This score indicates that you believe your church is at:

- **Level Five (90-100):** *Steadfast and assertive*
  —We can help the church sustain and innovate for greater influence.

- **Level Four (71-89):** *Striving for quality*
  —We can help the church advance to the next step.

- **Level Three (51-70):** *Secure and faithful*
  —We can help the church take the next step towards full commitment.

- **Level Two (31-50):** *Scratching the surface*
  —We can help the church overcome its challenges and move forward.

- **Level One (20-30):** *Struggling to move forward*
  —We can help the church organize and strengthen its efforts.

At Bridge Ministries, Inc. (BMI), our PrayerMatters services are designed to help churches and individuals improve and/or sustain their prayer lives. We can help your church get to the next level and beyond. Visit us at *www.BridgeInnovators.com* to learn more about our 40 Days of Prayer Initiative (40-DPI), to schedule your free 30-minute discovery session with our Founder, Dr. Hugh Wesley Carrington, or to book him to launch your 40-DPI.

PART I SCORING GRID				
Section One	**Strongly Agree**	**Agree**	**Disagree**	**Strongly Disagree**
Prayer is the fundamental biblical principle that should guide a church's activities (its ministries and programs).	2.5	2	1	0.5
The church's prayer life (its commitment to prayer) can positively impact the surrounding community.	2.5	2	1	0.5
The level of spiritual growth in a church can be strengthened through corporate prayer.	2.5	2	1	0.5
Prayerless Christians (church members) can impede the proper functioning of a church.	2.5	2	1	0.5
A prayer strategy should lead the spiritual, membership, and financial growth strategy for a church.	2.5	2	1	0.5

Section Two	**Yes**	**No**
Is there a spiritual environment in your church that supports prayer and prayer related activities?	2.5	0.5
Does your church have a prayer champion(s), i.e., someone with a profound understanding of the importance of prayer in God's house (your church) and supports it?	2.5	0.5
Does your church view individuals, practices, and/or things that are hindering its spiritual growth and development as a threat?	2.5	0.5
Is your church recognized by the community as a place of prayer?	2.5	0.5
Is the attendance at prayer meeting worship service significantly lower, when compared with other worship services?	0.5	2.5

HOUSE OF PRAYER INDICATOR ASSESSMENT

Section Three	Strongly Disagree	Disagree	Agree	Strongly Agree
Cultivating and maintaining an organizational culture and worship structure where consistent corporate and personal prayer is the norm, is practiced at my church.	0.5	1	2	2.5
In my church, prayer plays a prominent role in the lives of members and chiefly in the lives of church leaders.	0.5	1	2	2.5
My church is not simply going through the motions, and focuses on genuine prayer and worship, week after week.	0.5	1	2	2.5
My church does not need to change its assumptions, ways of thinking about, and approach to prayer.	0.5	1	2	2.5
My church's primary function, first and foremost, is to be a house of prayer.	0.5	1	2	2.5

Section Four	Yes	No
Is prayer worship?	2.5	0.5
If your church were to schedule a prayer meeting service and a game night, would the attendance at game night be better?	0.5	2.5
Is prayer included in the mission and vision statements of your church?	2.5	0.5
Are the church's ministries adding spiritual value to the community?	2.5	0.5
Does your church spend quality time in prayer at committee and planning meetings?	2.5	0.5

PART II SCORING GRID				
Section Five	Strongly Disagree	Disagree	Agree	Strongly Agree
I think prayer, as a central worship practice, has been removed from the center of my church.	2.5	2	1	0.5
The legacy of prayerlessness in my church is negatively impacting our surrounding community.	2.5	2	1	0.5
I've witnessed that there is a correlation between my church's spiritual weakness and its lack of corporate prayer.	2.5	2	1	0.5
Prayerless Christians (church members) are impeding the proper functioning of my church.	2.5	2	1	0.5
A prayer strategy is not leading the spiritual, membership, and financial growth strategy for my church.	2.5	2	1	0.5

Section Six	Yes	No
Is the level of unity (oneness, one accord) great among members at your church?	2.5	0.5
In your church, is more time allocated for Bible study, singing and/or preaching, when compared to time spent praying?	0.5	2.5
In your church, are the youth and children excited about prayer?	2.5	0.5
Do all of the worship services in your church reflect prayer as a priority?	2.5	0.5
Are there individuals, practices, and/or things in your church preventing it from moving forward spiritually?	0.5	2.5

HOUSE OF PRAYER INDICATOR ASSESSMENT

Section Seven	Strongly Agree	Agree	Disagree	Strongly Disagree
Churches should cultivate and maintain an organizational culture and worship structure where consistent corporate and personal prayer is the norm.	2.5	2	1	0.5
Prayer must play a prominent role in the lives of church members and chiefly in the lives of church leaders.	2.5	2	1	0.5
Churches should avoid the pitfall of simply going through the motions, week after week, when it comes to genuine prayer and worship.	2.5	2	1	0.5
Churches that are serious about prayer, usually change their assumptions, ways of thinking about, and approach to prayer.	2.5	2	1	0.5
The church's primary function, first and foremost, is to be a house of prayer.	2.5	2	1	0.5

Section Eight	Yes	No
During the last 3 months, have you preached or heard your pastor preach a sermon on prayer?	2.5	0.5
Does your church have a weekly prayer worship service where prayer, and only prayer, is the focus?	2.5	0.5
Are your members and visitors excited about prayer?	2.5	0.5
Does your church have and use prayer request cards and/or a prayer box?	2.5	0.5
Does your church have a vision for prayer (i. e. a clear awareness of what can and will happen when you and other members pray)?	2.5	0.5

Notes to the Reader

Bridge, Inc.

Visit us at *www.BridgeInnovators.com* to learn more about our companies and the services that are designed and available for churches and religious organizations.

At Bridge, Inc., we provide innovative solutions for more abundant living. Our member companies include:

- **Bridge Ministries, Inc.** (BMI)
  —PrayerMatters

- **Bridge Consulting, Inc.** (BCI)
  —Organizational Learning & Development

- **Bridge Research, Inc.** (BRI)
  —Research & Evaluation

- **Bridge Press, Inc.** (BPI)
  —Book Concept Development and Publishing

Coming Soon!

PrayerCharged is a ten-minute daily devotional that will charge your day and change your life forever.

Have you ever had a car where the battery ran down? As you know, when this happens you lose power. In most cases, all that's needed is a jump—a charge. Sometimes it's a simple spark that restores power, and other times a longer charge is needed. *PrayerCharged* will provide the necessary spark to restore spiritual power in your personal life and in your church.

Stay connected with us and be one of the first to know when this new book, *PrayerCharged: Your Ten-Minute Daily Devotional*, is released.

NOTES TO THE READER

Available Now!

About the Author

Hugh Wesley Carrington, Ph.D., is founder of Bridge, Inc. Hugh helps organizations optimize performance through training and development of their members at all levels and the streamlining of organizational processes. He is an accomplished, dynamic speaker, and blends his love of education, the study of people, and research into his process-driven approach to organizational learning and development.

Before anything else, Hugh is a Christian who believes in the power of prayer. In addition to leading Bridge, Inc., Hugh is currently also an Adjunct Professor at Long Island University in the School of Business, Department of Social Work, and the Department of Sociology and Anthropology.

Hugh has held several departmental positions in local churches of a denomination that numbers almost 20 million worldwide. He is a frequent presenter at local churches and related events and has had the opportunity to observe how we as Christians approach prayer. He has had the opportunity to implement what he teaches, including his signature House of Prayer process, and knows that it works.

Hugh holds a M.S. in Human Resource Management, a Ph.D. in Sociology, a M.A. in Higher Education Administration, and a BA in Marketing Education. Hugh resides in Stamford, Connecticut, and is married to the former Maxine Cenac. He is the adoring father of a college sophomore, Serina Jordan Carrington, and a preschooler, Hugh Wesley Carrington, Jr.

www.ingramcontent.com/pod-product-compliance
Lightning Source LLC
Chambersburg PA
CBHW031055080526
44587CB00011B/696